DECISION AND DESTINY

DECISION AND DESTINY

By

GEORGE ARTHUR CLARKE

Author of "The Purpose and the Hour"
and "The Pathway to the Cross"

Published by

The Blakiston Company

PHILADELPHIA

Distributed by

Fleming H. Revell Company

NEW YORK AND LONDON

To Those of Our Fellowship
in Service in Many Places for
God, for Loved Ones, and for Country

FOREWORD

THAT the destiny of men, of nations, indeed of our whole civilization, rests ultimately upon the decisions of individual men and women is a sobering and a challenging thought. In *Decision and Destiny* Dr. Clark drives home this conviction with overwhelming force.

In a series of sermons, built around eighteen Bible characters and illustrated by many references to contemporary life, he shows how a given decision, at a focal point in a man's life, determined the destiny not only of that one man, but also of the community, the world, and the day in which he lived. Here are Jacob and the decision to rise above self, Daniel and the decision to claim religious liberty, the Rich Young Ruler and the decision to play safe, Saul of Tarsus and the decision to obey—all vividly presented with a rich background of biography and world events, past and present. David and Nehemiah, Washington, Churchill, and Niemœller, all move across these pages. The sermons are scholarly, yet modern and alive as this morning's newspaper. Pertinent to our own lives, they help us to see how our individual choices are pregnant with destiny for ourselves and for others.

Here is Biblical and expository preaching at its noblest and best. A most valuable book for the man who wants to know his Bible, its historical background, and its great heroic characters; a wealth of illustrative material for the Church school teacher; a suggestive and inspiring approach

7

for the minister who needs a preaching tonic. A book to read, to study, and to enjoy.

JOSEPH CHANDLER ROBBINS,
President of the Northern Baptist Convention and member of the staff of Andover-Newton Theological School.

Wollaston, Massachusetts.

CONTENTS

9

I

JACOB

The Decision To Rise Above Self

"Thy name shall be called no more Jacob, but Israel."
—Genesis 32:28.

Twins are sometimes almost identical. Indeed, they may
be so much alike that even parents must distinguish them
by the slightest differences in smiles, voice tones or gestures.
Jacob and Esau, however, were not identical twins. They
were about as different from each other as two boys could
be. Esau loved the outside sporting and hunting life; Jacob
remained at home. Esau was the favorite of his father, who
loved the venison brought home from the hunt; Jacob was
the favorite of his mother and even learned to cook. Esau
was easy-going; Jacob was meditative. Esau placed little
value on his rating as the senior son with the birthright;
Jacob was greatly concerned about his place in the family.
Esau went the easy and obvious way; Jacob was a man of
thought and drive and initiative. Esau was transparent and
forthright; Jacob was reserved and a schemer.

Jacob Was Selfish. He well deserved the name of "Supplanter." On two outstanding occasions he gained what he
wanted at the expense of Esau. One day Esau came in from
the hunt, tired and hungry. The hunt had apparently been
a failure that day. At home he found Jacob just completing
the preparation of a great pot of steaming food, the pottage,
very likely containing meat and vegetables. When he asked
for a portion of it, the trickster at once proposed the un-
equal bargain of the pottage for Esau's birthright. That

birthright involved all that went with the senior son's place in that patriarchal society. Esau accepted the bargain, for, easy-going as he was, the satisfaction of immediate needs meant more to him than a distant heritage. "The birthright for a mess of pottage." Esau is not alone in making such a bargain. Each one of us makes such a deplorable bargain whenever some immediate desire is satisfied at the expense of some distant value. A night at a "Cocoanut Grove" has often cost the birthright of great values which are distant and so undervalued.

The other occasion on which Jacob carried through a scheme for personal gain at the expense of Esau was when Isaac knew that he was approaching death. Esau, as the senior son, was to receive the patriarch's blessing. Isaac told his son Esau to go for venison for a final meal together and the blessing of his son. Off he went. Rebekah, with her favors for Jacob, informed him of what was to happen. Together they worked swiftly at a disguise. Two kids from the flock were killed and prepared as venison. Jacob's hands were covered with skin of kid and he was dressed in the clothes of Esau, the hunter. Isaac thought the voice was Jacob's, but the hands were those of Esau. The trick worked. Isaac gave to Jacob the blessing that belonged to Esau, saying,

"See, the smell of my son
Is as the smell of a field which the Lord hath blessed:
And God give thee of the dew of heaven,
And of the fatness of the earth,
And plenty of grain and new wine:
Let peoples serve thee,
And nations bow down to thee:
Be lord over thy brethren;
And let thy mother's sons bow down to thee:
Cursed be every one that curseth thee,
And blessed be every one that blesseth thee"
(Genesis 27: 27-29).

That settled the matter of the inheritance. Jacob had completely supplanted Esau. It was natural that when Esau came home and found out the selfish trick which had been played on him that he took deep offense. Esau knew then the significance of having sold his birthright. When Esau asked for a blessing from his father, Isaac could only give a secondary one and said (Genesis 27: 39-40):

"Behold of the fatness of the earth shall be thy dwelling,
  And of the dew of heaven from above;
  And by the sword shalt thou live, and thou shalt serve thy
    brother;
  And it shall come to pass when thou shalt break loose,
  That thou shalt shake his yoke from off thy neck."

The selfishness of Jacob had gained its end at the expense of Esau.

Selfishness is the root of a whole progeny of sins. Indeed, it may be identified as the root of the weed of sin. In the action of war where men are risking everything the sin that men despise beyond everything else is *selfishness*. The judgment of the soldier is not far wrong. Certainly the selfishness of Jacob was the root of lying, deceit, stealing his brother's birthright, and overreaching. "Take heed to thyself."

A Prosperous Man. Yet Jacob was a very prosperous man. For fear of the vengeance of Esau, Jacob went about four hundred miles to the northeast to the lands of Laban, his uncle. Esau had threatened to murder Jacob. At the home of Laban, over a period of fourteen to twenty years, Jacob became the head of a household of his own. Leah and Rachel and the two women servants were his. He had eleven sons and a daughter. He had men servants and maid servants. He had cattle and sheep and camels. Then he planned to return to Canaan. True to his tricky nature, he stole quickly away instead of planning a decent departure.

Two problems confront inquiring minds who come to this story.

One is: Why do the evil prosper? That was the problem of Jeremiah, stated in Jeremiah 12:1, "Wherefore doth the way of the wicked prosper?" That is also the problem of the 73rd Psalm. That is often the problem of honest men who go on their honest way and live on meager returns. No final answer has come. Jeremiah and the author of Psalm 73 both had visions of God which gave them strong answers that the end of the story would bring satisfaction for the righteous, while the evil man's foundations would not stand the test of time. It is the short view of things that sees evil winning. The basic philosophy of Hitler's Nazi regime is the deliberate use of the lie in large political and national undertakings. It got away to a speedy start, for a lie will ride round the earth while truth is getting its boots on. But truth does get its boots on at last, and time is with truth.

I once heard Dr. Russell Conwell preach in his own pulpit in Philadelphia. Someone had written him a letter asking the question, "Can the Lord save a liar?" The result was that Dr. Conwell preached on "Liars." He told of outstanding liars in the city of Philadelphia and what their end was. Then he told a Civil War story. A single track railway ran between Chattanooga and Atlanta. Traffic was one way for certain hours and the other way for certain hours. However, in a pressing situation a train started off schedule against traffic. It made a station and backed into a siding to let traffic pass. It made a second station in the same way. Then it came to a third and backed into a siding. But the siding was not long enough for the train. The engine and two cars were still on the main track. The traffic was coming against it—it was caught. Said Dr. Conwell, "The lie will work once, twice, the third time—or more—and then when you back into a siding of ridiculous explanation, you find you are hopelessly against the traffic and you are caught and exposed." The Machiavellian philosophy of expediency and the deliberate lie in national affairs is failing Hitler.

14

Even his own people are "getting wise," and in the world of nations he and his regime are caught and hopelessly discredited.

The other problem facing the inquiring mind is, Why did God choose a man like Jacob to lead a great cause? The answer cannot be complete. This is plain, however: Esau lacked appreciation of values and lacked initiative. In a modern city like Boston or New York he probably would be classed among the likeable playboys. Jacob was serious, a thinker, a leader, and he was aggressive. God has to use the man who is available. But before He uses Jacob He deals with him.

Our Past Catches Up With Us. The story of Jacob reminds us that our past catches up with us. It did with Jacob. When he moved south from Padan-aram it was to learn that Esau was moving north from Edom. Jacob was in the deepest distress. He came to the great crisis of his life.

Jacob had to decide whether he would go on with his trickery to its inevitable crash or whether he would rise above self into a life worthy of a son of God. Something within him told him that his great hour of decision had come. It was a decision that would spell out destiny for himself and his age and his people.

A Repentant Man. Jacob repents. When night came on and his people had an altar over the brook Jabbok, Jacob remained behind and spent the night with God. The struggle with God was personified by the use of the picture of a physical wrestle which Jacob had with another physical being. The ancient writers of the Hebrews were past masters in the art of presenting spiritual truths in physical pictures and by personification. That literary device is at its best here. It is the literary mould used so tellingly by John Bunyan. To read Bunyan is to meet physical beings on an earthly roadway. They become so real that one must recall the fact that Pilgrim is on a spiritual adventure and in

15

body really never leaves his own home. Such a physical picture tells the story of the struggle of the soul of Jacob. The soul of Jacob struggled with God all night. Victory came in the morning. Jacob won. The repentant man became the regenerated man. It was a new birth. Jacob, in this Old Testament story, had the experience of the new birth which Jesus taught to Nicodemus in the New Testament.

The trickster became the man of God. The spirit of God said, "Thy name shall be called no more Jacob, but Israel." The Supplanter had become the Servant. But he was crippled in order to be crowned. He carried the reminder of his his former life until his death.

A Sense of Mission. From now on we see a man with a sense of mission.

It is fitting that Israel and Esau met in a brotherly reconciliation. Each man went to his own task, and they were brothers in God.

Israel is now the leader of a great adventure. The names of his sons will be the names of the tribes of Israel. The outreach of this man's life in his own nation and in our modern world is the story of a man serving in a great mission under God.

It is significant that the most famous well of Palestine became known as Jacob's well. We have no stories about Jacob going about digging wells. Isaac, his father, did that. However, this Israel dug wells in a far more significant way. He was one of God's great pioneers.

In England there is a little town named Hannawell. The story of the village is that long ago the daughter of a leading man of the place, named Hannah, died. The father planned to erect in her honor a monument in the village square. On the advice of the rector of the church the plan was changed. The rector learned that the people very badly needed a great central well. The great well was dug in the center of the village. It had a fine stone parapet and a spacious seat. Ever since the people have come to the well for fresh water from the unfailing spring.

Well-digging may be something quite different from digging down to a spring in the earth. Well-digging may be digging into the resources of life that people might be refreshed and strengthened. A good book may be such a well; a beautiful song may be such a well; a painting, a friendship, a society, a club, a piece of social planning, a church service—all these may be wells, and by the same token we may all be well-diggers, and our fellow-mortals may be refreshed.

A few years ago I received a Christmas card from a close friend, Dr. F. W. Patterson, now President of Acadia University. It was headed "Wells And Monuments." It read

"It is better to open a well than to erect a monument."

> *When you open a well, you tap the resources of nature; you invite the waters to fill it.*

When you erect a monument, you challenge the forces of nature; you defy the weather to destroy it. When you erect a monument, men ask, "What did he do that this should be erected?"

> *When you open a well, men ask, "Who was he that made it possible for us to drink and be refreshed?"*

When you erect a monument, you perpetuate your name.

> *When you open a well, you perpetuate your influence.*

When you erect a monument, men will question your merit.

> *When you open a well, your merit is assured; only your name may be uncertain.*

When you erect a monument, you attempt to change the world's center.

> *When you open a well, you minister to the world's need.*

17

When you erect a monument, you mark your grave.

When you open a well, its gushing waters assure your immortality; you live again in lives made better by your presence.

The monument is the symbol of selfishness; the stars in their courses are pledged to destroy it.

The well is the symbol of unselfish service; every resource of God is pledged to fill it.

That is the message of Jacob. It is the story of the selfish Jacob who, by the divine grace, became the servant of God, Israel, by whom all the nations of the world are blessed.

We, too, may rise above self. Indeed we must "rise on stepping stones of our dead selves to higher things." Theodore Monod has expressed it this way:

> "O, the bitter shame and sorrow
>   That a time could ever be,
> When I let the Saviour's pity
> Plead in vain, and proudly answered,
>   'All of self, and none of Thee.'

> "Yet He found me; I beheld Him
>   Bleeding on the accursed tree,
> Heard Him pray, 'Forgive them, Father!'
> And my wistful heart said faintly,
>   'Some of self, and some of Thee.'

> "Day by day His tender mercy,
>   Healing, helping, full and free,
> Sweet and strong, and ah! so patient,
> Brought me lower, while I whispered,
>   'Less of self, and more of Thee.'

> "Higher than the highest heaven,
>   Deeper than the deepest sea,
> Lord, Thy love at last has conquered;
> Grant me now my soul's desire,
>   'None of self, and all of Thee.' "

II

MOSES

The Decision To Be Free

"I will send thee unto Pharaoh, that thou mayest bring forth my people."—Exodus 3:10.

THERE are three great documents of the Christian era which bear on the question of human liberty. For Americans the document which is native to our soil is the Declaration of Independence. It was the formal declaration of American political independence issued by the Continental Congress on July 4, 1776. To the people of Britain the document which is native to their soil is the Magna Charta. It embodied the demands of the barons and was granted by King John in 1215 at Runnymede. That document, however, extended its benefits to freemen, and mainly to the landholders. The landworkers were not free from arbitrary demands, or arrest. The "villains," who comprised three-quarters of the entire population of England, were still feudal serfs, the property of the lordly landholders. It did not give to these people, through elected representatives, the powers to plan and control taxation, or trial by jury. The barons themselves were the men mainly benefited by the Magna Charta. The liberty of the people and their real exercise of power came in the struggle of the House of Commons with Charles I. After that the voice of a free people began to speak with power.

Behind these two national documents, the Declaration of Independence and the Magna Charta, there is a third document, a religious one. It is the letter of Paul to the Galatians, a basic declaration of liberty of soul, the liberty of the sons of God, to whom liberty comes through the ministry of the Great Liberator, Jesus Christ, and Paul says, "Stand

19

fast therefore in the liberty wherewith Christ hath made you free and be not entangled again with the yoke of bondage." That letter of Paul was surely never revised. It is the hot, flaming declaration of a soul standing erect and affirming his liberty in the name of God. That letter of Paul is basic to and grandparent of both the Magna Charta and the Declaration of Independence. If both those political documents were blotted out, something like them would rise again from Paul's letter to the Galatians.

However, in the book of Exodus there is not so much a declaration of liberty as an adventure in liberty. Surely here we are walking on ground of real history. If the years of slavery in Egypt were not historically real, the Jewish people would long since have repudiated it as fiction or legend.

The hero of that story is Moses, who decided that he and the people would be free.

Revolt Against Oppression. The resentment of the souls of the people is epitomized in the revolt of Moses. Although he had been nurtured in a princely environment, "blood was thicker than water" and his heart was with the oppressed people of his race. They were slaves. When they wanted better working conditions, the response was that they would still produce the same amount of bricks, but for the output no straw would be provided. They must now gather their own straw. Rameses the Second marched them in slave bands in the project of massive building programs. Archæology has discovered the great Tell Rotah storehouse built by him with Hebrew slave labor.

Moses saw the horrible misery of that slavery. One day, when he thought that nobody was looking, he killed an Egyptian who was particularly abusive to a Hebrew. The following day he interfered with two Hebrews who were in a fist fight. The better fighter replied, "Who made thee a prince and a judge over us? Thinkest thou to kill me, as thou killedst the Egyptian yesterday?" It was time for action.

Moses' interference on behalf of the slaves would be known by Pharaoh and he would slay Moses, the freer of the slaves. Thus Moses flees to Midian. The wide wilderness and the extensive pasture land was a refuge for a hunted man.

An Experience of God. In Midian Moses had the second period of his education, his preparation for a great task. It was a long, long trek across the barren wilderness to the tents of Midian. When in later years he was with the Hebrew tribes in the wilderness he must have recalled his lonely trek, how he lived on handfuls of berries gathered by diligent searching and was grateful for a mouthful of water found by removing a rock. Was it during that trek that he learned by hard experience where to look for a spring? The story of that lonely trek has not been told. He left Egypt and he was in the tent of Reuel, priest of Midian. Like Jacob in the tent of Laban, he became part of the group, tending flocks and herds, and he gained a wife, Zipporah. A few verses later the name of Moses' father-in-law is given as Jethro. The term father-in-law was often loosely used and might refer to many relationships by marriage. Was it that on the death of Reuel, Jethro succeeded him as priest of Midian? Or does Dr. Moffat give the real explanation? Dr. Moffat regards the use of the name Reuel as an editorial alteration of name. The real name is Jethro. Jethro, father-in-law of Moses, is not only a protector for Moses, he is his friend, teacher and adviser. Indeed, in his later wilderness experience with the tribes Moses is advised by Jethro in matters of administrative justice.

It is in Midian that Moses has a new experience of God. The Midianites were also descendants of Abraham and his wife Keturah. Living the open life of the wide pasture lands, they kept in simple purity their worship of Jehovah. In Egypt the Hebrews inevitably had been influenced by the different culture of the people in the Nile Valley. In Midian

21

Moses has a vivid experience of God which is a determiner of his own destiny and the destiny of a race.

It happened while he was tending the flocks beyond the desert. In the extreme heat of Midian it was not uncommon to see a bush heated to the point where it burst into flame. But, nearby, Moses saw a bush aflame, as though on fire, but not consumed. Dr. Kirtley Mather has pictured it as a bush of red berries or red leaves flashing back the rays of the setting sun so that it was like flaming fire. Dr. S. Parkes Cadman has expressed it this way: "The familiar story of the burning bush is the literary expression of a profound spiritual experience which transformed the inmost being of a man." * The Hebrew writer had a remarkable genius for expressing spiritual truths in physical pictures. Without the language of science, psychology, and philosophy, he wrote and spoke in pictures. The "sea of glass" in Revelation is never mistaken for actual glass, but for what is intended, a description of what the writer had often seen, a bit of the Mediterranean smooth as glass, reflecting the sun. John Bunyan took over the use of physical pictures to express spiritual truth and used it with grand effect in *Pilgrim's Progress,* so that at times we forget that Pilgrim in body really never left home at all. It is all a created physical picture of a spiritual adventure.

Thus Moses, attracted by a glowing bush, reflecting the light of the setting sun, draws near. He is ready for a spiritual experience. For Mrs. Elizabeth Barrett Browning

> "Earth's crammed with heaven;
> And every common bush afire with God;
> But only he who sees, takes off his shoes—
> The rest sit round it and pluck blackberries." **

* From *The Prophets of Israel,* p. 8, by Dr. S. Parkes Cadman. Used by permission of the publishers, The Macmillan Co., New York.

** From Book VII, "Aurora Leigh," by Elizabeth Barrett Browning.

Moses knew that God was near. He must approach God with reverence. Indeed, if we ever are to learn from Him as we ought, reverence is necessary. It is not a matter of whether or not shoes were actually removed. It was a matter of a reverent spirit. God was all about him and he was in God's holy presence. Any spot of earth beside any bush can be exactly that when the attitude of the spirit is one of sincere desire, reverence, and receptivity. Moses qualified for his experience of God.

There beside the bush Moses learned that what he had already suspected to be true was God's will and way for him. He must actually, under God, be the deliverer of his people. "I will send thee unto Pharaoh that thou mayest bring forth my people the children of Israel out of Egypt."

That was not the first time that Moses had felt that he must have a part in that adventure of freedom. But now he faced the great decision of his life and the destiny of a race turned on it.

An Honest Self-Estimate. Moses has brought himself under examination. He doubted his own powers. There is that rod—a physical picture again—grand in its significance. Here the Hebrew writer is superb. What does the rod mean? Surely, nothing but the native powers which Moses possesses. Let those powers run loose and undisciplined, out of hand, and they are serpents that sting, poison and kill. That is true of all our human powers. Undisciplined, out of hand, they destroy. The power to get may become sheer banditry, whether by the use of guns or cruel economic controls. A power to speak may, out of hand, become a cruel, cursing tongue, an affliction to all who have to endure it. James had some real reason for describing the awful havoc wrought by the unbridled, undisciplined tongue. The power of love, out of hand, undisciplined, may become riotous license and licentiousness. A human life is an equipment of native powers. Let them loose—out of hand—and they are deadly serpents.

23

God's word to Moses is, "Take that serpent by the tail," and when Moses takes it in hand it is a rod. Surely the thing stands out as clear as a church steeple. God is saying, "Moses, you have tremendous powers. Never mind the lack of speaking ability. Aaron can do that. But you have real powers to lead. Out of hand, they are serpents. Taken in hand and disciplined, they are a rod by which you can walk in hard places, with which you can strike in desperate circumstances, with which you can direct, now that the people need a leader. Moreover, Moses, I am with you. When the people ask you for your credentials, tell them that you met with God, who said 'I Am That I Am,' and that 'I Am' has commissioned you to lead them."

Responsibility Accepted and a Destiny of Freedom. The next time we see Moses he is in Egypt. He speaks to the people and instructs them in preparation. He meets with Pharaoh, stubborn, despotic Pharaoh, and in a succession of interviews, like the repeated refrain of a great song, says, again and again, "Let my people go, let my people go, let my people go." At last, when the first-born of the land are dead, from the palace to the humblest home on the flats by the Nile, Pharaoh lets the Hebrews leave.

The rest is the struggle to make good this liberty. The Red Sea, the wilderness, the Tabernacle, the Decalogue, the entrance into Canaan, the mistakes and achievements—these are all part of the struggle for freedom. In all that adventure Moses appears in massive proportions. Jethro, his father-in-law, the Midianite, is, at one point at least, a close adviser. Moses became so great that when he died the place of his grave was a secret with God. Why hide the grave? Surely it was because the grave of such a great one might become a shrine, a substitute altar. When Michelangelo wrought his great statue of Moses, he portrayed strength and greatness in every muscle and feature. Then he added the touch of two horns above his forehead. Not God—but greatness beyond all men who surrounded him.

Freedom is not a gift. Freedom is a reward. It was a reward for Moses and his people, who struggled and fought for it. It is a reward for the individual who will struggle for it. A free nation cannot be built up from individuals who are slaves to sin and are debased in their own characters. Professor William George Jordan of Queen's University, Kingston, Ontario, put it this way:

"At each moment of a man's life he is either a king or a slave. As he surrenders to a wrong appetite, to any human weakness; as he falls prostrate in hopeless subjection to any condition, to any environment, to any failure, he is a slave. As he day by day crushes out human weakness, masters opposing elements within him, and day by day recreates a new self from the sin and folly of his past—then he is a king. He is a king ruling with wisdom over himself. Alexander conquered the whole earth—except Alexander. Emperor of the earth, he was the servile slave of his own passions." *

That man who in his own character has achieved freedom as a son of God is the hope of the nation—and the only hope of the nation—to become and remain free.

It comes right down to this, always: Freedom is based at last on a right relationship with God. Of my noble-souled predecessor in the pastorate of the First Baptist Church of Malden, Dr. William Quay Rosselle, it was written,

"He walked with truth, and welcomed larger truth;
He lived by truth, nor paltered with untruth.
Thus he was free, as God's own sons are free,
Who seek God's truth, His life in all to see."

That truth is personal in the life of Jesus. He bids us go along with Him. In that companionship, with Him, the Truth, the Saviour, the Lord—struggling on with Him, face

* From *The Kingship of Self-Control*, p. 9. Published by Fleming H. Revell Co., New York.

25

forward in battle with every enslaving thing, we can know the freedom of the sons of God. As freemen of free spirits we can make our nation clean and free, for Satan himself will take his hands off when, as sons of God, we say it, mean it, and fight for it—"Let my people go."

Over three thousand years ago Moses decided for freedom in Midian. Today we are seeing that freedom tested by a satanic effort to enslave us again. But, as the great-souled Abraham Lincoln put it, "This nation, under God, shall have a new birth of freedom." Like Moses, we draw near the burning bush, with shoes removed from our feet, with souls bowed in reverence, with minds ready to learn and hands ready to do. The Eternal "I Am" is with us in Him who says "I Am The Way." The Promised Land of Christian righteousness and liberty is our destiny.

> "Jesus, still lead on
> Till our rest is won;
> Heavenly Leader, still direct us;
> Still support, control, protect us,
> Till we safely stand
> In our fatherland."

III

JOSHUA

The Decision To Serve God

"And if it seem evil unto you to serve the Lord, choose you this day whom ye will serve; whether the gods which your fathers served that were beyond the river, or the gods of the Amorites, in whose land ye dwell: but as for me and my house, we will serve the Lord."—JOSHUA 24:15.

JOSHUA was one of the twelve scouts who had gone on ahead into the land of Canaan to secure information about the

26

country and the people. Joshua and Caleb were the two who reported that while there were fortified cities and well-armed soldiers, the land was fertile and productive, and they were well able to go in and possess it.

Joshua becomes commander-in-chief of the Hebrew fighting men by the authority of Moses. It is Joshua who leads the actual invasion. At Gilgal, meaning "Rolling" (Joshua 5:9), the twelve stones carried from the Jordan were erected into a cairn, perhaps a circular cairn, the reminder to Israel from the Lord, that "this day have I rolled away the reproach of Egypt from off you." For that reason that place of the cairn was called Gilgal—Rolling.

Did not George Washington and his men come to their Gilgal at Valley Forge? It is fitting that a beautiful chapel now adorns that historic camp of the Revolutionary army, and that on the altar of the chapel appears George Washington's prayer, which reads:

"Almighty God, we make our earnest prayer that Thou wilt keep the United States in Thy holy protection, that Thou wilt incline the heads of the citizens to cultivate the spirit of subordination and obedience to government and entertain a brotherly affection and love for one another and their fellow citizens of the United States at large. And, finally, that Thou wilt most graciously be pleased to dispose us all to do justice, love mercy, and to demean ourselves with that charity, humility and pacific temper of mind which were characteristics of the Divine Author of our blessed religion, and without a humble imitation of whose example in these things we can never hope to be a happy nation. Grant our supplication, Father, we beseech Thee, through Jesus Christ our Lord. Amen."

Jericho and Ai are conquered under the strong leadership of Joshua. If any sculptor had undertaken to portray the character of Joshua, surely ruggedness, courage and honesty would be expressed in a soldier's physique.

The purpose of this half hour with Joshua is to see and

hear him in a covenant conclave with the tribes of Israel, dealing with the major question of their loyalty to the God who has been leading them through the wilderness into a national home.

The Strength of a Man or Nation Is in that Man's or Nation's Loyalties. The place of the national conclave is Shechem. Shechem is in the center of the area occupied by Joshua's tribe, Ephraim, as Ephraim, in turn, is central in the area occupied by the twelve tribes of Israel.

Shechem was already a sacred and meaningful shrine for the people. It was at Shechem that Abraham had built an altar when he penetrated the land into which he had gone as a pioneer of faith. There is "the oak of Moreh" (Genesis 12:6-7). It was at Shechem that Jacob built an altar on his way back from Padan-Aram (Genesis 33:20). It was there that Jacob hid the foreign gods under the oak (Genesis 35:4). Shechem was the sacred spot for the burial of the body of Joseph (Joshua 24:32). Not far from the site of the tomb of Joseph was dug the well that became known as Jacob's well (John 4:11).

The valley of Shechem was an ideal place for a national conclave. The valley is about 1800 feet above the sea-level and it is fertile and inviting. To the north stands Mount Ebal, its slope ascending another 800 feet. To the south is Mount Gerizim, with slopes which also ascend some 800 feet above the valley. The valley itself narrows toward the east and rises until it comes to a "shoulder" or "saddle" of land, which makes a watershed. It is that which gave the place the name Shechem. Rainfall at that point divides and watercourses make their way to the east toward the Jordan and to the west toward the Mediterranean Sea. At the eastern end the ascending valley of Shechem narrows to a distance of a little more than 300 yards. There, with Ebal and Gerizim for walls, the trees for pillars, the sky for a roof, the rocks for cathedral chairs, the sun for light, and the birds for music, Shechem, a natural amphitheatre, is a grand temple amid the hills.

Joshua calls the tribes to Shechem. They are making progress in the conquest of Canaan. It is time for a national convocation in the presence of God. The story of that convocation is told in Joshua 8:30-35. Very likely the tabernacle was erected for that solemn conclave. The ark of the covenant would be there. An altar of unhewn stones was erected. Burnt offerings were offered to God. Then, on a suitably prepared plaster covering the stones, Joshua very likely wrote the ten commandments. Around the ark are gathered the Levites. Part of the great conclave have their backs to Mount Ebal. Half of them have their backs to Mount Gerizim. In the midst of the valley stands Joshua. They had often heard his voice in military commands. Now they heard that clear, strong voice read the whole law of Moses, with its blessings and its cursings. The people in a thunderous response say, "Amen."

The people in a great national convocation, with the land partly conquered, but battles yet to be fought, have committed themselves to their God. To God they would render the homage of worship and God alone they would serve.

In such a spirit the people were at their best. They were united in a great struggle for a national home and freedom. "Idols" had little place then. In a similar mood, fighting America is seeing impatient people bring to justice the gambling racketeers of cities like Boston. We are not fighting to make America the happy hunting-ground of callous, calculating, unpatriotic gangsters and racketeers.

The Perils of Making Good a Victory Are Worse Than the Perils of War. As the battles in Canaan moved toward victory, Joshua saw what our world has been sadly learning, that the perils of making good a victory are more deadly than the perils of war.

Did not we see that in that period between the victory of

1918 and the outbreak of another war in 1939? What we called a peace was not even a good armistice. The period of time between 1918 and 1939 was marked by fun, fury, and foolishness. As people have spoken with some fondness for "the gay 90's," now they are scornful in referring to "the twinkling twenties." It was a cynical, shallow, supercilious, and "debunking" age. It was the field day of the playboy. A wisecracker, with very little in the way of wise plans, could become mayor of New York. The debunking biographer sold his caricature of George Washington and Henry Ward Beecher to a public which demanded that everything be said and done smartly. We thought we were on an ever-ascending way of solid prosperity. We were in a light-headed dance of destruction. On came the depression and then came the thunderclouds over Europe, and over China. Those thunderclouds spread over the Pacific and the Atlantic, and only when the storm broke over our very heads did we learn through our skins what we were too dull to learn through our minds. Our false gods of smartness, cynicism, and debunking had failed us.

As victory in Canaan became a reality and as the tribes were taking possession of their national home, Joshua saw the weaknesses and the vices appearing which would mean losing the peace after winning the war.

Reality in Religion the Great Assurance for Liberty and Stability in the Peace beyond the War. Joshua saw clearly that he must plan for the peace beyond the war. Already, and perhaps, not altogether out of view, in the experience of war he saw the weaknesses and vices that would wreck the peace. Those weaknesses and vices would be exaggerated when military victories had removed the dangers from enemy armies.

Thus there is the second convocation at Shechem. The Levites, the tribes and their leaders are in the amphitheatre of the fertile valley. The tabernacle and the ark are again there. Joshua, the warrior, with decades of campaigning behind him, is now nearing the century mark in age. Yet he still is strong and keen in mind. Joshua has three requirements, which if met, would make the future strong in liberty.

False Gods are to be put away. Those false gods were sometimes the actual teraphim, small doll-sized idols such as those carried by Rachel from the house of her father, Laban. When Laban came searching for his household gods, Rachel sat upon them and later Jacob buried them beneath the oak in Shechem. Similar gods were now in the possession of the people, a left-over from past worship. Such gods must be destroyed. The idols might be idols of the mind. Superstition can be an idol of the mind. Superstitious fears paralyze the mind. Seamen often have a superstitious fear of the albatross. Yet Bomber Pilot Harold Dixon and his two companions of *The Raft* shot and ate the albatross which had alighted on the stern of their little rubber boat.* That was "putting away" the idol of superstition. It was an evidence of faith in God. Ambitions can be idols of the mind. Having won military victory, rugged, aggressive men would shoulder their way to place and possession at the cost of the weaker, and ribald pleasures would demoralize the life of the tribes of Israel. Joshua was not mistaken in his insight into the tendencies among the people. Those very things, false gods, idols of the mind, later did bring the people to a place where Isaiah, Amos, and Micah condemned them for their godlessness, their injustice and their immorality. "Put away the false gods."

Sincerity in worship is another thing which Joshua required. Joshua established near "the oak," likely the oak of Moreh, "the sanctuary of the Lord." At the first convocation at Shechem, Joshua had built an altar. Sanctuary and altar —these call the spirit of man to worship. Now Joshua says,

* *The Raft,* by Robert Trumbull, p. 70. Published by Henry Holt and Company.

"Fear the Lord," which fear, as Dr. Moffat puts it, is "to revere" the Lord. That matter of reverence is so very vital. Reverence is the exercise of the capacity to appreciate superior quality in the object of adoration and the aspiration to become like that in character. The moral value of worship cannot be overestimated. What evangelism seeks to accomplish through preaching is also accomplished through sincerity of worship. Let a man go alone, or as a part of a group, to the sanctuary and bow before the altar of God, whether that altar be visible or invisible, in a stone temple or in a vale at Shechem, and the inevitable result is an experience of cleansing, clarification of vision and a sense of dignity as a son of God. "Be still and know that I am God." "Worship the Lord in the beauty of holiness." The man who has attained the attitude of reverence, and sincerely and intelligently worships, is very apt to be a bulwark of freedom and stability in the state; for by his very experience of worship he aspires toward and struggles after the life that is on the proper plane for a son of God.

> "Satan trembles when he sees
> The humblest saint upon his knees."

Faithfulness in the Service of God. The third thing Joshua requires is sincere service of God. With such a man there is no longer a line of demarcation between the secular and the sacred, for all life is sacred to him and all people are sacred. That man's work is sacred. It was on that basis that George Washington approached all life. Religion penetrated all of life. Thus he said, "True religion affords to government its surest support." Thus it was that while it was a task under God to lead the Revolutionary armies as commander-in-chief and to serve two terms as president of the newborn America, it was just as sacred a task under God, when he had retired to Mount Vernon, to serve on a petty county jury when it came his turn.* That is real religion and that is Christian democracy. That is "serving the Lord" by serving one's fellowmen.

A modern counterpart of that convocation in the vale of Shechem was the convocation of the Scotch Covenanters in Greyfriar's Churchyard, in Edinburgh, on February 28, 1638. That covenant of faith in and liberty in the God of Jesus Christ was brought before the assembly. One by one the covenanters signed it. Many of them opened veins in their arms and dropped the pen in their own blood. The sheepskin with those blood-written signatures may still be seen in Edinburgh.

Such a covenant we are again called upon to make with God. It must be individual, one by one, in order to make it strong for all. Said Joshua, "As for me . . . ," and then came his family and then came the tribes, who vowed anew their loyalty to God.

That was mobilizing the religious faith and the moral intelligence and strength of the people for the struggle to make good the peace. Plans will be made and discarded and new plans will be made. Deeper, however, than plans must be the attitude of spirit that will give no place to false gods, will worship God in reverence and will serve God in sincerity.

Jesus is the Joshua of the New Testament. The names are the same. Jesus is our adequate Redeemer and Leader.

"He that followeth me shall not walk in darkness, but shall have the light of life."

* *George Washington,* by Woodrow Wilson, p. 312. Published by Harper and Brothers, New York.

IV

KING SAUL

The Decision To Disobey

"Behold, to obey is better than sacrifice."—I SAMUEL
15:22.

SAMUEL, the seer, was the last Israelite judge. Samuel was
utterly autocratic in religion. He was more autocratic than
prophets like Elijah and Elisha. He was the absolute head
of a theocratic administration. Any disobedience to Samuel
was considered by Samuel as disobedience to God. That is
the theory of a theocracy. On this occasion of the battle
with the Amalekites Saul and his people disobey Samuel in
saving sheep and oxen for their own use and for sacrifices at
Gilgal. Samuel interprets that as disobedience to God. One
cannot help but have some sympathy with young King Saul
when he dared to disobey Samuel. More than that, one
questions whether disobedience to an autocratic Samuel
really is disobedience to God. Our modern Protestantism
does not grant for a moment that the thought of any one
man or any group of men can be imposed upon us as "the
will and command of God." That position we give to Jesus
alone. But we instinctively and correctly rebel against religious autocracy by any individual preacher, priest, or
bishop, or even by any association, synod, or assembly. The
capacity and right of the individual to get through to God
himself, "the priesthood of the believer," is a deep truth we
act upon whenever we refuse to conform to any attempted
religious autocracy.

The work of Saul was a valuable foundation for the work
of David. Saul's kingdom, which stretched along the banks
of the Jordan perhaps fifty miles from east to west and 150
miles from north to south, became something like a united

nation. Saul's military leadership in his rescue of the men of Jabesh-Gilead and at Micmash marked him as a soldier of ability. The attainments of Saul were a foundation for the further development under David.

Was disobedience to Samuel disobedience to God? At least, we of this age of Protestantism demand the right of individual judgment—"soul liberty."

Obedience to what we are sure is the will of God for us is another thing. Knowledge of the will of God for us individually may come through contemplation of a need which we can meet, conference about that situation with other men who are deeply concerned about it, and through quiet waiting before God in meditation and prayer. Then to disobey is perilous. We disobey at the cost of leaving undone an important task and at the peril of our very souls.

When the preacher in Samuel said, "To obey is better than to sacrifice," he uttered a profound truth, bearing in mind that the obedience is to God, not necessarily to another human.

To Obey is Better than Sacrifice because the offering of a sacrifice may easily be a matter of correct technique without any bearing on quality of life or sincerity of spirit. Indeed, spiritual implications and values might be utterly lacking. Correct technique in offering a sacrifice often came to be regarded as religious righteousness. Let the place and time of the sacrifice be correct; let the formula of language be correct; let the genuflections be correct; let the music be correct; let the animals or birds offered in sacrifice be correct, and with that perfect technique in sacrifice attained, religious righteousness had been attained.

When Jesus came to the temple, that was the situation which confronted Him. There were sacrifices aplenty and the ritual was elaborate and correct. The temple never displayed more gorgeous splendor. The spirit of the priests, however, was another matter. Jesus charged them with turning the House of God, His own House, into a profitable market, and a money-changing center where high rates of interest enriched a degenerate priesthood. Jesus called those who controlled those sacrifices hypocrites and whited sepulchres. Jesus wanted genuineness of spirit at the temple, and it was because Jesus demanded of the temple priests that they really fulfill their mission as ministers of God to a needy people instead of robbing sincere and innocent worshippers that they planned the death of our Lord. Surely, for those priests "to obey God would have been better than sacrifice."

To Obey God is Better than Sacrifice because the offering of a sacrifice might easily be a matter of escaping divine judgment rather than living by a spirit of justice. It was precisely that abuse of sacrifice which aroused the ire of the prophets who denounced the sacrifices with burning words.

Thus Isaiah says: "What unto me is the multitude of your sacrifices? saith Jehovah. I have had enough of the burnt-offerings of rams, and the fat of fed beasts; and I delight not in the blood of bullocks, or of lambs, or of he-goats" (Isaiah 1:11).

Thus Jeremiah says: "Your burnt-offerings are not acceptable, nor your sacrifices pleasing unto me" (Jeremiah 6:20).

Thus Hosea says: "I desire goodness, and not sacrifice; and the knowledge of God more than burnt-offerings" (Hosea 6:6).

Thus Amos says: "I hate and despise your feasts, and I will take no delight in your solemn assemblies. Yea, though ye offer me your burnt-offerings and meal-offerings, I will not accept them; neither will I regard the peace-offerings of your fat beasts. Take thou away from me the noise of thy songs; for I will not hear the melody of thy viols. But let justice roll down as waters, and righteousness as a mighty stream" (Amos 5:21-24).

Thus Micah says: "Wherefore shall I come before the Lord and bow myself before the high God? Shall I come before him with burnt-offerings, with calves of a year old? Will the Lord be pleased with thousands of rams, or with ten thousands of rivers of oil? Shall I give my first-born for my transgression, the fruit of my body for the sin of my soul? He hath showed thee, O man, what is good; and what doth the Lord require of thee, but to do justly, and to love mercy, and to walk humbly with thy God?" (Micah 6:6-8).

Thus says the Psalmist: "Thou delightest not in sacrifice; else would I give it. Thou hast no pleasure in burnt-offering. The sacrifices of God are a broken spirit: a broken and a contrite heart, O God, thou wilt not despise" (Psalm 51:16-17).

In all this it is the preacher, the street preacher, the prophet, who is demanding genuineness at the temple, where formality in sacrifice had become an escape from divine judgment and the spirit of justice was absent. "To obey is better than sacrifice."

To Obey is Better than Sacrifice because it costs more, and obedience brings that obedient man into the fellowship of the redemptive sufferings of the love of God. That man shares in the suffering love of God whose purpose is our human redemption. To purchase doves or a sheep or an ox and surrender that gift at the sacrificial altar is a cheap matter of religious observance compared with the cost of identifying one's life with the redemptive purpose of God. That identification of spirit with the spirit of God means inevitable suffering. It is of the very essence of such purposeful love that it suffers. It is at that point that suffering becomes noble; it goes beyond duty and becomes a privilege.

What a roll of honor of such souls could be called? Isaiah, Jeremiah, Amos, Micah—these men might easily have excused themselves from danger and suffering. They might have said that the matter of religious leadership was the responsibility of the temple and the priests. They might have taken the attitude that since the temple could not minister to them they would simply remain away and practice their religion as a private matter or among small, like-minded groups, quietly. But they walked out into the open streets of Jerusalem, uttered their denunciations, spoke their messages about real religion being a matter of life—a matter of righteousness, mercy and justice. They paid the cost in suffering.

John the Baptist paid the cost of obeying God. He might have remained "a voice crying in the wilderness," but he struck straight at the palace of Herod Antipas and became a voice rebuking an unfaithful ruler. And John's courage cost him his life. But it was his life he lost, not his soul. The world, however, gained a knowledge of what real religion ought to be and must be.

The story of the Christian Church from the days of Jesus until this hour is replete with the names and records of men and women who, in obedience to God, have suffered and have put the world forever in their debt, for their suffering has meant our liberty.

Dr. Albert Schweitzer might have proven to the last syllable the proposition that he should remain with his music and gain a great deal of money from his books on Bach and organ recitals in London and New York, and with part of a great income send six doctors to Africa instead of his lonely self. But Albert Schweitzer knew what was the way of God for him and from Lambaréné goes out a Christian message and a Christian influence that no six substitutes could create or send forth. Albert Schweitzer is right. "To obey is better than sacrifice."

To Obey is Better than Sacrifice because men who have at great personal sacrifice obeyed the will of God have been the makers of progress for the Kingdom of God. There are

38

places where careful business methods apply in the work of the Christian Church, and we need the business of the church attended to with competence and care. But there are areas where those business standards do not apply. They did not apply when the church at Antioch prayed over what was made known to them as the will of God. Paul and Barnabas had been preaching in the strategic center of Antioch for about a year. In that great city of 200,000 people multitudes were turning to Jesus Christ by the preaching of these men, yet right then the Holy Spirit made it known that these two men must leave Antioch and pioneer the Christian work in the West. The church acted on the truth that "to obey is better than sacrifice." They did not raise a fund to send six substitutes. They put their hands on Paul and Barnabas, prayed over them, dedicated them and sent them forth. The sequel is the Christian Church in Europe, Great Britain, and America.

When David Livingstone had nearly worked himself to death in Africa, he was found by Sir Henry M. Stanley. Stanley tried to persuade the worn and wasted Christian hero to retire, to go home. But Livingstone replied, "I must remain and finish my work." "To obey was better than sacrifice."

When Adoniram Judson was suffering untold indignities in Burma a Spanish collector of customs advised him to return to his native New England, but he decided to remain and introduce Burma to his Christ. Has not Burma by now learned the difference between the righteousness and mercy of Jesus Christ and the cruelty or an Oriental despotism that has broken in upon them? The great chapter of Judson's adventure to Burma has yet to be written. Jesus Christ and His religion will now stand in such sharp contrast to Japanese cruelty that the future in Burma is assured for Jesus. The story of Adoniram Judson and his accomplishments says, "to obey is better than sacrifice."

Young Dr. Wilfred Grenfell heard D. L. Moody in London. At first he was amused. Then he became serious. Afterwards he was saying to himself, "I must either take my religion seriously or else give it up altogether." The sequel is the North Sea, Newfoundland, and Labrador, and progress for the Kingdom of God. Dr. Grenfell did not remain in London to gain a fortune and send six substitutes. He went himself. "To obey is better than sacrifice."

This is the truth that emerges—that the man who obeys becomes himself the "living sacrifice." That is the language of the Apostle Paul. He broke away from the temple altar in order that he might obey God. Now he could never be contented with a sheep slaughtered and burnt upon an altar of stone. It was nothing less than putting himself at the disposal of the will of God. That is what a "living sacrifice" is. It is not the burning of a sheep's dead body, but all the powers, talents, and faculties of a strong, alert, purposeful man brought into harmony with God and put at the disposal of His will. It means devoted work year in and year out. Paul put into words what the older prophets were struggling to express when they denounced insincere burnt-offerings and demanded the realities of righteousness and justice and mercy in religion. Paul's immortal statement of it is, "I beseech you, brethren, by the mercies of God that you present your bodies a living sacrifice, holy, acceptable unto God, which is your reasonable service." It needed Jesus in a man's experience to enable a man to state it like that.

"To obey is better than sacrifice."

V

DAVID

The Decision To Be Somebody

"And David said unto Ahimelech, And is there not here under thy hand spear or sword? And the priest said, The sword of Goliath the Philistine, whom thou slewest in the vale of Elah, behold, it is here wrapped in a cloth behind the ephod: if thou wilt take that, take it: for there is none other save that here. And David said, There is none like that; give it me."—I SAMUEL 21:8-9.

HISTORY and tradition have dealt very severely with Saul and very generously with David. Saul was not such a wretched person as a combination of facts has pictured him. And David was not so perfect as another selected combination of facts has pictured him. Each man was a mixture of virtues and weaknesses.

The very things, for instance, for which Samuel condemned Saul are the things which David does and for which he goes unmolested and for which he is honored. Saul offers burnt offerings and peace offerings to God in a religious service, before his men go into battle (and does it for the reason that the seven days appointed by Samuel have passed and Samuel has not arrived) and for that Samuel tells Saul that he has done foolishly and that the kingdom would be given to another (I Samuel 13:8-14). David offers burnt offerings and peace offerings, dressed in the linen ephod of a priest, and for that the king goes unmolested and it is recorded to his honor (II Samuel 6:12-19). When Saul fought the Amalekites he and his people kept a quantity of supplies which had been captured, and for that act Samuel said that Saul was to be rejected and dethroned (I Samuel 15:10-26). When David fought the Amalekites he, too, saved great quantities of supplies and distributed them among the elders and among his friends in villages of Judah. That is recorded to David's honor (I Samuel 30:18-31).

The work of King Saul, a pioneer in attaining national unity, ought to be more fairly appraised. As a matter of fact, the work of Saul in bringing a central part of the country into something like unity was a foundation for the more extensive work of King David. Perhaps David could never have accomplished so much without the work of Saul.

We see the young man David and the seasoned warrior King Saul meeting on three significant occasions. One is when Saul wants a musician to soothe his troubled spirit. Saul was a sick man. A competent modern doctor would have identified his trouble as nervous exhaustion, developing into a condition of mental depression—melancholia. The music of David, a "cunning player on the harp," brought temporary relief. David apparently goes back and forth between the pastures of his father, Jesse, at Bethlehem and the court of King Saul at Gibeah.

The second meeting of King Saul and David is on the occasion of the duel with Goliath. Jesse had sent David to the scene of the battle with the Philistines to take "parcels" to "the boys at the front," and to inquire about their health. David had three older brothers in active service there, Eliab, Abinadab, and Shammah (I Samuel 17:13-14). Eliab accused David of vanity of heart—a boyish curiosity to see a battle. The well-known duel between David and Goliath followed. Surely David knew he had all the advantage. The armor of Saul was a burden to him. "His staff and his sling." If there had to be maneuvering for position, the agile strength of David could soon tire the cumbersome giant. David, moreover, could fight at a distance. Goliath could never toss a javelin so far or so swiftly or so accurately as David could sling one of those smooth, round stones from the brook. David had practiced in the pastures and had sunk stones into the foreheads of lions and bears. Goliath never saw the stone coming. It crashed into his forehead. Goliath was beaten. David leaped from the place of a shepherd musician to that of a national hero. He is received into Saul's home.

The next time we see Saul and David, Saul is in a condition of deep mental depression and is wild with jealousy. The people have been praising David. The women were singing

> "Saul hath slain his thousands,
> And David his ten thousands."
> *(I Samuel 18-7).*

Repeated attempts on David's life result in David leaving the king's house. Saul might be "the Lord's anointed," but David did not propose to be killed even by a king. Michal, David's wife, and Jonathan, Saul's son, assist David to escape.

David Decided that He was Going to Live and Be "Somebody" worth while and do something that would count for the people and for God. Already he was a marked man of God, as the story of the anointing of David at the home of his father, Jesse, tells us. Abraham Lincoln came to that hour of his life when he decided that he would hold a rendezvous with destiny. He would be somebody and do a worth-while thing. Mrs. Crawford, the wife of a man for whom young Abraham Lincoln worked, would ask: "What do you want to be now?" His answer was invariably, "I'll be President." Mrs. Crawford would answer, "You'd make a purty President with all your tricks and jokes. Now, wouldn't you?" He would then declare: "Oh, I'll study and get ready, and then the chance will come." * He did study, and at Springfield, Illinois, he was to speak at the courthouse in an election campaign. George Farquer was a leading citizen of Springfield. By changing political affiliation

* *The Early Life of Abraham Lincoln,* by Ida M. Tarbell, p. 62. Published by S. S. McClure, New York.

he had secured for himself the position of Register of the Land office at what was then a large salary. Seven Whigs and seven Democrats were engaged in the debate. The young Lincoln surprised the audience by his mastery of debate. Although George Farquer was not a candidate himself, he felt that he had to help out the candidates of his party. He was an able speaker and was swaying the audience. But he made the fatal remark, "This young man must be taken down, and I am truly sorry that the task devolves upon me."

Young Abraham Lincoln had been thinking quickly. He remembered that in coming into Springfield he had seen the large house of George Farquer surmounted by a lightning rod, a new device. Abraham Lincoln claimed the right to speak in his own behalf and said, "The gentleman commenced his speech by saying that 'this young man,' alluding to me, 'must be taken down.' I am not so young in years as I am in the tricks and trades of a politician but," said he, pointing to Farquer, "live long or die young, I would rather die now than like the gentleman, change my politics, and with the change receive an office worth three thousand dollars a year, and then feel obliged to put a lightning rod over my house to protect a guilty conscience from an offended god." *

A young David had slain a political Goliath with sling and stone. Abraham Lincoln had stepped out into the world determined to be somebody and do a worth-while deed. Thus did young David depart from the house of Saul for life in the larger world. He would live to be "somebody."

David Had Splendid Qualities to Invest in the Enterprise of Being and Doing. There is no better description of those qualities of character which were his strength than that given by one of the young men of Saul's court, who directed the

* *The Life of Abraham Lincoln,* by Isaac N. Arnold, pp. 46, 47. Published by A. C. McClurg, Chicago.

attention of the troubled and depressed Saul to the shepherd-harper, David. He said, "Behold, I have seen a son of Jesse the Bethlehemite, that is cunning in playing, and a mighty man of valor, and a man of war, and prudent in speech, and a comely person, and the Lord is with him" (I Samuel 16:18). Surely those qualities, when looked at, are the very timber of character. "A cunning player,"—he has taken time to attain a degree of culture in music. How often a soldier who can "play well" can sit at a piano and lead his comrades in music and songs that mean so much as a cure for "the blues." "A mighty man of valor," David had fought his fears until he was brave. Courage is not the absence of fear. It is the defeat of fear. To be fearless may mean that a man has no appreciation of the meaning of a dangerous situation. Fearlessness may be no more than animal boldness. The courageous man is the man who really appreciates the meaning of a situation, who knows what is involved and has deliberately fought down the fears of his mind and disciplined himself into the determination to endure. That is courage. "A man of war," David had practiced fighting against lions and bears when he was alone in the pasture lands. He knew how to handle the weapons of the fighting man. "Prudent in speech," David was no careless talker. He thought and then spoke. He was wise. He was a man of good judgment. "A comely person," David had lived life in the open. His very skin glowed with health. His eye was alive with interest and intelligence. In vain we ask for a perfect physical picture of David. Michelangelo, however, has said in stone, in his statue of David, exactly what the young man at Saul's court said, "A comely person." David was a good person to look at as he walked about among his fellows. The glow and health and honesty of the outdoor life of the pasture lands were on him.

Young David was rebuked often enough for his venture.

King Saul rebuked him to the point of hunting him like a partridge, to kill him. Nabal, the rich farmer of the south country, rebuked him and compared him to a runaway servant. But David had fine and strong qualities of character and he was moving toward a destiny.

David Lloyd George, Prime Minister of Great Britain in the first world war, had a fight to get out into the world where he lived his life and did his work. In Wales he had anything but a good start. His father had died when the lad was but eighteen months old. That meant a home where struggle and frugality were constantly known. But Mrs. William George had a brother, a shoemaker, named Richard Lloyd. "Uncle Lloyd" was a lay preacher as well as a shoemaker. He undertook the protection of his sister and her children. The early education of David Lloyd George was watched over by Uncle Lloyd, who kept the boys at school two years beyond the ordinary time. David showed signs of determination to be somebody. To be articled to a lawyer demanded a standard of education which the local school could not provide. He must know more French and Latin. Uncle Lloyd knew neither French nor Latin. Then he would learn and learn with David. Together they explored French and Latin. Together at last they went to Liverpool, where David passed the examination at St. George's Hall. At Portmadoc he was articled to a lawyer. David Lloyd George kept a diary. When he was eighteen years of age he visited London and was taken to the House of Commons. When he returned home he made this entry: "I will not say but that I eyed the assembly in a spirit similar to that in which William the Conqueror eyed England on his visit to Edward the Confessor, as the region of his future domain." In some way the town paper heard of the dreams of the young man of Wales. In their columns they teased him. Then he made another entry: "Perhaps it will be gratified. I believe it

46

depends entirely on what forces of pluck and industry I can muster." *

Culture, courage, skill in combat, wisdom in speech, physical health which glowed, and companionship with God —these qualities are what made Abraham Lincoln, David Lloyd George, and David of Israel. When a man decides to be somebody he must, by the same token, be somebody who has strong potentialities of character to offer to that world of people into which he ventures.

When David Made His Venture into Life He Took God into the Reckoning. Anyone reading the story of David could select dark pages of David's mistakes and sins. How honest the Bible is. It does not make a man perfect by presenting virtues only. Neither does it make a man offensive by presenting vices only. David had both. But he constantly came back to God for counsel. How splendidly his sense of God appears in his chivalry. On two occasions he might have killed King Saul with a single blow. In a cave where David was hidden in the darkness and Saul was at his mercy, David cut the skirt from his robe, but spared the life of "The Lord's anointed." Then, in the open, with Saul at a distance, he held up the piece of the robe and appealed to King Saul to live at peace with him. For a while the king did (I Samuel 23:17-22). Then the man-hunt was on again. This time it was the wilderness of Ziph. Saul and his men were asleep on the hill of Hachilah. Saul was in the inner camp, surrounded by the wagons. His spear was driven into the ground at his head. Abner was on guard—or supposed to be. But Abner was asleep. David took with him Abishai and entered among the sleeping soldiers of King Saul. He came to the side of the sleeping king. Abishai said, "Let me smite him to the earth at one stroke, and I

* From *The Prime Minister,* p. 42, by Harold Spender. Used by permission of the publishers, Hodder and Stoughton, London.

47

will not smite a second time." But David said, "Destroy him not: for who can put forth his hand against the Lord's anointed?" David had a deep sense of God and took Him into the reckoning (I Samuel 26:9).

When the wars were over and David was reigning in Jerusalem he took occasion to inquire for anyone left of the house of Saul to whom he could do kindness. He found Mephibosheth, the son of Jonathan, a man lame in both feet. To this member of the house of Saul David showed mercy and gave him a place at the king's table as well as provision for a home of his own (II Samuel 9:1-13).

At the very beginning and at the end of his adventure into life David is seen consulting God and seeking to honor Him.

See David as he goes on that early visit to Nob, to the abode of the priest Ahimelech. The young man is fleeing for his very life. The priest gives to David the sword of Goliath, which was standing near the priest's own vestment, the sword which David himself had taken from the Philistine giant. The priest also gave to him the very shewbread that was before the Lord—the holy bread. What sort of pledge did David make when he left with that bread to sustain his strength and that sword with which to fight his way? (I Samuel 21:1-9). That early decision to live and be somebody who would do a worth-while thing led him to his destiny in God. At last the nation is strong and free. One of the last desires of King David was to build a temple for the worship of the most high God. The purpose was good, but because he was a man of war, it had to be left to another.

Surely the matter of most basic importance for us at this and all times is sincerely to take God into the reckoning. From the line of David comes that great Word of God that became flesh. We repentant humans, torn and bleeding from our own prodigal behavior, can, if we will, find God in Him, Jesus. In Jesus we can know God, find our way into the life with God and become worth-while persons and nations, doing our part even yet in the fuller realization of the Father's redemptive purpose.

> "Hail to the Lord's Anointed,
> Great David's greater Son!
> Who in the time appointed,
> His reign on earth begun!
> He comes to break oppression,
> To set the captive free;
> To take away transgression,
> And rule in equity."

VI

NAAMAN

The Decision To Have Faith

> "Then went Naaman down and dipped himself seven times in Jordan, according to the saying of the man of God: and his flesh came again like unto the flesh of a little child, and he was clean."—II KINGS 5:14.

A LITTLE Hebrew slave girl makes a remark that eventually means much to Naaman, the commander-in-chief of the army of King Benhadad of Syria. When the army of Benhadad had raided Israel, among the captives was a little maid who became the servant of Naaman's wife.

> "A chance remark, or a song's refrain,
> And life is never the same again.
>
> "A whispered 'Be brave,' to our fellowmen,
> And they pick up the threads of hope again.
>
> "Thus never an act, a word, a thought,
> But with some unknown importance is fraught.

49

"For small things build up eternity,
And blazen the way for a destiny."

Thus an incidental remark of a little Hebrew captive maid blazens the way for a better destiny for Naaman, the great soldier. The description given of Naaman is, "He was a great man with his master, King Benhadad; he was also a mighty man of valor, but he was a leper." That terrible merciless "but." It is like the butt end of a soldier's rifle that can come crashing into the face of an enemy in close combat. How often that is said in deadly judgment of a person. A man is mentioned for a post of responsibility and in that committee meeting one committeeman says, "Yes, he is a man of good ability—but," and then follows the revelation of some leprous spot in the man's record, which puts him out of the running. A woman is mentioned for some place of leadership. And again some committeewoman says, "Yes, she is capable and willing—but," and then follows the picture of an unlovely trait of character that ends the consideration of her name. "Naaman was a great man, but he was a leper." Turning the negative, destructive "buts" of life into positive, constructive virtues is the task of every day and of all the years.

The little maid said, "Would that my lord were with the prophet that is in Samaria! Then would he recover him of his leprosy." That remark of the maid to her mistress was repeated to Naaman and carried to King Benhadad. Benhadad was a man of action. He sent Naaman off with a party and packhorses, carrying ten talents of silver, and six thousand pieces of gold, and ten changes of raiment, coin and goods to an estimated value of $50,000. He gave Naaman a letter to Jehoram, king of Israel, stating that he wished Naaman cured of his leprosy. Jehoram was distressed, and rent his clothes, saying "Am I God, to kill and to make alive, that this man doth send unto me to recover

50

a man of his leprosy? But consider, I pray thee, and see how he seeketh a quarrel against me."

That visit did not disturb Elisha, the prophet. He said, "Let him now come to me, and he shall know that there is a prophet in Israel." Naaman, with his men and packhorses, goes to the humble house of Elisha.

The rest of the story is that of reaching a decision that meant a happy destiny for Naaman. But in the process he is to be seen in four distinct moods.

A Mood of Anxiety. The first mood is that of anxiety. Naaman's leprosy had not developed far enough to prevent him carrying on with his work, but it was a real handicap and a source of constant anxiety. The disease was considered incurable and it was distressingly progressive. No wonder leprosy has been used as the illustration of sin. It is contageous, progressive and deadly. It requires the attention of God.

Leprosy has had the attention of God through the consecrated work of consecrated science. The story of Father Damien is one of the noble chapters in the approach of Christian mercy to the leper.

The story of Alice Ball is one of those chapters of superb human devotion. It has been known for a long time that chaulmoogra oil is beneficial where cases of leprosy have not developed too far. But the heavy chaulmoogra oil was difficult to use. This scene of heroic devotion was in the efforts for lepers on the Hawaiian Islands. Dr. Victor Heiser was using chaulmoogra oil. He must have it in finer and more concentrated form. He wanted the refined, powerful essence of the oil for injections. The chemistry department of the Hawaiian University undertook the work. A young Negro woman, Miss Alice Ball, was assigned to the laboratory task of securing the essence. She succeeded in securing the finer essence, but grew sick herself while at work. She went to California to regain her strength. The partial success of the essence of chaulmoogra oil suggested a great achievement ahead. A yet finer essence must be secured. Miss Alice Ball went back to her work. She produced that finer essence. A few years ago leprosy was called an incurable disease. Today the disease can be halted among those who are reached soon enough, and they can go about their work. But how about Miss Alice Ball? The young Negro woman sickened again, beyond recovery, and passed away.* The vicarious suffering of a great devotion is written in golden letters in all the story of human progress. It is read in no nobler form than in the battle to defeat leprosy.

No wonder Naaman was worried. A worried man is not apt to be a patient man. Naaman was anxious about himself.

An Angry Mood. Now we see Naaman in an angry mood. He and his equipage of men and horses, bearing a valuable gift, are before the door of Elisha. A servant of the commander-in-chief of the Syrian army notifies the preacher of Israel that the great man has arrived. Elisha is not disturbed by the supposed greatness of Naaman. He sends out a servant with the message, "Go wash in Jordan seven times and thy flesh shall come again to thee, and thou shalt be clean."

Naaman's sense of importance was offended. He went up "the miff tree." That is just a human weakness with most of us. We love to have "a fuss" made over us. People enjoy a little or more extended personal attention. The evil of it is that when folks get to the point where the ego grows so important they are unhappy if they do not constantly receive attention and they are hurt when other busy people are too occupied to give it to them.

I have sometimes wondered what Elisha was doing when Naaman called. Was he preparing the sermon for the next

* From "Curing Leprosy in Hawaii," *The New York Times Current History,* 1921, p. 770.

Sabbath? Was he right in the middle of a manuscript? Was he held by the demands of some caller who in turn would be hurt if he left him or her to give attention to the foreigner? At any rate, the response was a message, "Go wash seven times in the Jordan."

Naaman was hot with resentment and anger. He went off with his equipage, in high dudgeon. He said to one of his companions, "Are not Abana and Pharpar, the rivers of Damascus, better than all the waters of Israel? May I not wash in them and be clean?" Naaman was in a rage. As a matter of fact, those rivers of Damascus were far better than the muddy Jordan. The river Barada, the Abana of Naaman, springs fresh and clear from Anti-Lebanon. It plunges wildly down the gorge of Wady Barada. At a distance of fourteen miles from Damascus it is joined by another stream, born of a gushing spring which doubles the volume of the clear waters of the Barada, the far-famed Abana of our story. The clean, fresh water of the Barada turns the valley through which it flows into a verdant paradise. Willow trees and poplars prosper, and rose bushes and berry bushes abound. Gardens are green because of well-watered soil. The homes of the peasants are in the midst of gardens. In the midst of it all is the never-failing Barada, supplying clear mountain water to garden and people alike. Then the river divides into seven branches, as though determined to give its every drop of water for the life of a countryside and a city. Apricot orchards thrive. Then the main current of the river enters Damascus, or rather Damascus has built itself along the banks of this main current. The city taps this stream for the water that is its very life. When the Barada leaves the city on the opposite side, it loses itself in a swampy area, fertile with reeds and rushes. Beyond is the desert. The Barada never reaches the sea. It literally dies to make Damascus. The waters that have come gushing from the side of Anti-Lebanon are fresh and clear. Naaman had bathed to his delight in the Barada. The waters of the Barada supplied his home and garden. "Are not Abana and Pharpar, too, better than all the waters of Israel?" Naaman was right, but Naaman was also wrong.

Naaman's servant said, in a daring remark of kindly rebuke, "My father, if the prophet had bid thee do some great thing, wouldest thou not have done it? How much rather then, when he saith to thee, Wash, and be clean?" Naaman's angry resentment began to cool. He cooled off in the same skin he got hot in. He repented. Nobody can force another man to repent of an angry, mistaken attitude and act. The man must change his mind himself. Naaman did. He returned to the bank of the Jordan.

A Humble Mood. Now we see Naaman in a humble mood. Indeed, until we can approach God in a mood of humility there is little possibility of God doing much for us. Pride and stubbornness put a barrier between the soul and God.

In a church which a group of us attended one summer Sunday morning, I heard again an elderly Scotch Presbyterian minister, to whom I had often listened with delight. That morning he was struggling to tell his people what humility is. After about twenty minutes, he said, "My people, do you know what I think humility is? It is just good manners in the presence of God." The Psalmist puts it this way, "Come, let us worship and bow down. Let us kneel before the Lord our maker." It is like the ancient knight entering a neighboring knight's castle by the small door. He must leave his warlike steed outside. He must take off his plume-crested helmet, lower his spear, and bow his shoulders, and then he can enter. Humility is such an approach to God —a reverent approach.

We read that Naaman was a man of valor. When he had once made up his mind about what was right, he never hesitated. Neither did he do things secretly or shamefacedly.

54

Thus Naaman walked steadily down the Jordan bank, praying as best he could to the God whom he did not know in a deliberate act of faith. Once, twice, three times, four times, five times, six times, and seven times he buried his leprous body beneath the waters of Jordan, and the hand of God touched him and Naaman was healed, and "his flesh came again like unto the flesh of a little child." "This is the victory . . . even your faith." That decision to have faith has everything to do with destiny. Said Jesus, in His most important affirmation, "Have faith in God."

A Grateful Mood. Now we see Naaman in a grateful mood. Once Jesus healed ten lepers, and only one returned to give thanks, and he was a Samaritan (Luke 17:11-19). Naaman, the Syrian, was grateful. He wanted Elisha to accept a generous gift, $50,000. Elisha refused. He was not selling the grace of God. It must have humiliated Elisha when later he discovered the disgraceful act of his servant Gehazi, who contrived to get money and raiment.

When Naaman learned that Elisha would take nothing from him, he asked Elisha for something. What a strange but interesting request. He said to Elisha, "I pray thee, let there be given to thy servant two mules' burdens of earth; for thy servant will henceforth offer neither burnt-offering nor sacrifice unto other gods, but unto the Lord." The idea was common to the day. Israel was the land of God. God belonged to the land. It was the very soil of God. Naaman wanted the two mules' burdens of soil to transport all the way to Damascus. That soil would be carefully placed in a protected spot. On that soil he would build an altar. At that altar he would worship God. To us God is the universal God and all soil is the soil of God. We may build our altar anywhere, and we may find Him and worship anywhere.

Naaman made an interesting remark about his official duties. At times officially he must enter the temple of Rimmon with his master, who worshiped his own Syrian god.

On such occasions he was the king's officer and must not make himself obnoxious. When he bowed at such times in the house of Rimmon, he wished the Lord's pardon. Thus the phrase, "bowing in the house of Rimmon," has a special meaning for us. The official attendance and respectful behavior of Naaman in the house of Rimmon apparently did not disturb Elisha greatly. He merely said, "Go in peace," and left Naaman without any condemnation. He trusted the grace of God which had healed Naaman to lead him on. God's grace would be sufficient. That attitude does not give us permission to play fast and loose with religious and ethical matters. Not at all. For one thing, God, we know now, is not local, but universal, and beside Him there is no God. We must in good conscience learn how to pay respect to any person of authority and at the same time maintain our loyalty to the God and Father of our Lord Jesus Christ. Polycarp, the Bishop of Smyrna, would not give the worship due to God alone to a deified Roman emperor. Certainly, we in our day will never give to a rampant race god or national god the place that belongs to God alone. We shall render unto Cæsar the things that are Cæsar's, but we shall not render unto Cæsar the things that are God's. It is that, at center, which is really the meaning of the global struggle in which we are now engaged.

This story has a strange climax. The man who came with leprosy went away healed. That was a destiny for him because he decided to have faith in God. It was faith in God, not the muddy waters of the Jordan, that healed him. But another man, Gehazi, a servant of Elisha, became a leper. Rather the leprosy that became evident in his body was the picture of the leprosy of deceit in his soul. The change in the soul of Naaman was more important than the change in his body. We all need that spiritual change. When Jesus was criticized for taking dinner with publicans and sinners He justified the fact that He was with them by saying,

"They that are whole have no need of a physician, but they that are sick: I came not to call the righteous, but sinners."

There is One who can heal and change us. He is the Christ of God.

> "The Great Physician now is near,
> The sympathizing Jesus."

VII

ISAIAH

The Decision To Preach

"Here am I; send me."—ISAIAH 6:8.

IF WE can get a glimpse of this majestic man and hear the echoes of his voice in his faithful, daring and loyal preaching we shall learn much. Isaiah was not recognized by the temple priesthood. They were all for the endless offering of sacrifices, and Isaiah was all against it. He was a preacher without a church—without a pulpit. But he was not a preacher without a congregation. He preached for nearly half a century in Jerusalem. His preaching place was the street.

If you can imagine a preacher in Boston so very different from all the others that St. Paul's Cathedral, Tremont Temple, King's Chapel, Park Street Church, Arlington Street Church, and Emmanuel Church unanimously closed their doors to him and he had to take a spot beside a mall of Boston Common as his outdoor church, that would be Isaiah. His ministry went on for well-nigh fifty years. He was different. He never said the safe thing; he always said the dangerous thing, for he asked for truth, and seeing it, stated it. It can hardly be said that he was popular with any group

57

for any length of time, and it is possible that the end of his life was just what a persistent tradition says it was, that he was sawn asunder by the order of the faithless, idolatrous, and cruel King Manasseh.

The preaching ministry of Isaiah was in the setting of cruel and intensive military attacks on Palestine. The first was during the reign of Ahaz, and it was led by Tiglath-Pileser, in 734-732 B.C. The second attack was led by Shalmaneser and Sargon in 725-720 B.C., which invasion saw the fall of Samaria in 721. The third attack was by Sennacherib in 701 B.C. Hezekiah is king at Jerusalem. Isaiah preaches confidence in God. The last attack by Sennacherib failed. This great Jerusalem preacher had continual military invasion of his land, the empty formalism of the temple priesthood, and the fears of the people as the permanent setting of his ministry. Isaiah had to match his faith against the fears and superstitions of a broken-spirited city.

The book of Isaiah, as we have it, is more than a book. It is a record of the preaching of at least three men, covering a period of at least three hundred years. Thus the book of Isaiah has well been called a "library" of preaching, the summary of preaching of men from 740 B.C., on for a period well beyond three hundred years. The first of these preachers is Isaiah of Jerusalem, whom we meet in this contemplation. He preaches before the exile. The synopsis of his preaching is to be found in the first thirty-nine chapters. A second preacher, the great Unknown Prophet of the Exile is heard in mighty sections beyond chapter forty. He preaches in Babylon during the exile. A third body of preaching, found in different parts of the library, the preacher or preachers unknown, belongs to a time beyond the exile. It is Jerusalem again. Let this not be considered any adequate statement concerning the literature of the book of Isaiah.

We are merely reminding ourselves that the preacher we are to meet now is the first of the group, that he preaches in Jerusalem, and that we hear echoes of his preaching in the first thirty-nine chapters of the book of Isaiah. He is a prince among preachers, a great mountain peak in a range of hills.

Here he comes, then, Isaiah, the aristocrat with very democratic habits. He has access to the palace of the king, but the priests have no place for him at the temple. He is a "voice crying in the streets." For three years, during which he is especially anxious to reach the heart of the people, so unresponsive, he goes without a top garment, and barefoot. For three years he goes around that way. Can you see him? I mean can you see him as though he is appearing in Boston, on the mall along Tremont Street, beside Boston Common? He has no coat. For three years he has been going without a coat, in his shirt sleeves. He has neither collar nor tie, nor hat. His shirt is open at the neck and he walks the mall beside Boston Common. There he begins to preach. The people gather. His voice is like the tone of a silver trumpet. He needs no loud speaker to help him. His voice carries, and it carries conviction of sin to the crowd who hear. There are priests on the edge of the crowd who would like to murder Isaiah. Can you see him? And can you hear him? He is in shirt sleeves and he is barefooted.

Isaiah Preaches on a Variety of Themes During that Long Half-century of Ministry! Perhaps we can do no better than attentively hear him—if we will listen—on some major themes.

Is it the question of temple sacrifices? The priests demand them of the people and they officiate at the altars. Isaiah sees no virtue in the streams of blood, the incense and the ritual. He is utterly against it all, and he says:

"Hear the word of the Lord [the people can see the smoke of the sacrifice opposite to them at the temple as he speaks].

. . . To what purpose is the multitude of your sacrifices unto me? saith the Lord. I am full of the burnt-offerings of rams and the fat of fed beasts, and I delight not in the blood of bullocks, or of lambs, or of he-goats. When ye come to appear before me, who hath required this at your hands, that you trample my courts? Bring me no more vain oblations; incense is an abomination unto me; new moon and sabbath, the calling of assemblies—I cannot away with iniquity and the solemn meeting. Your new moons and your feasts my soul hateth: they are a trouble unto me. I am weary of bearing them" (Isaiah 1:10-14).

Is it the frivolity of the women of Jerusalem? The spirit and attire of empty show? A Jerusalem "Cocoanut Grove?" Did Isaiah blame the women's lavish and voluptuous tastes as responsible for the men's hard and dishonest business ways in order to get the necessary money? Surely Isaiah must have been *persona non grata* with the women of Jerusalem, or at least with a section of them. Hear him as he says:

"Because the daughters of Jerusalem are haughty, and walk with stretched forth necks and wanton eyes, walking and mincing as they go, and making a tinkling with their feet: therefore the Lord will smite with a scab the crown of the head of the daughters of Jerusalem. In that day the Lord will take away the bravery of their anklets, and the crescents; the pendants and the bracelets; the sashes and the perfume boxes; the rings and the nose jewels; the festival robes, and the mantles and the shawls; and the satchels; the hand mirrors and the fine linen, and the turbans and the veils. And it shall come to pass that instead of sweet spices there shall be rottenness; and instead of a girdle a rope; and instead of well set hair, baldness; and instead of a sash a girding of sackcloth: instead of beauty, branding" (Isaiah 3:16-24).

The women of Jerusalem were not very far from that, for Jerusalem women would soon be roped-up slaves on their way to Babylon. And the voice of Isaiah preached on—a "voice crying in the street."

Was it extortion and ill-gotten gain? Did Isaiah charge the women of Jerusalem with making such demands for finery and luxury and extravagant and profligate entertainment that their husbands were driven to desperate measures to pay for it all? Says he:

"Woe unto them that join house to house, and lay field to field, till there be no room. Of a truth many houses shall be desolate, even the great and fair. Ten acres of vineyard shall yield ten gallons. Eleven bushels of grain shall yield one bushel in return" (Isaiah 5:8-10).

Says this Jerusalem street preacher, in effect, "You cannot be unjust to your brother and your brother's home and escape punishment—the chickens will come home to roost. There will come a day when for you the wages of your sin will be death to your own prosperity and plenty."

Is it a matter of trusting to superstition and material power? Isaiah says:

"Because ye have said, We have made a covenant with death, and with hell are we at agreement; when the overflowing scourge shall pass through, it shall not come nigh us; for we have made lies our refuge, and under falsehood have we hid ourselves: Therefore thus saith the Lord God, Behold I lay in Zion for a foundation a stone, a tried stone, . . . and the hail shall sweep away the refuge of lies. . . . When the overflowing scourge shall pass through, then ye shall be trodden down by it. . . . The bed is shorter than a man can stretch himself on it; and the covering narrower than he can wrap himself in it. . . . Now therefore be not scorners. Give ear, and hearken to my voice" (Isaiah 28:15-23).

Isaiah would have them know that their superstitions were too weak and unreal to meet their needs as the sons and daughters of God. As for their trust in material power, says Isaiah:

"Ye have said, We will flee upon horses. We will ride upon the swift. Thus saith the Lord, In returning and rest ye shall be saved; in quietness and confidence shall be your strength" (Isaiah 30:15-16).

Is it the fact that religion which is real and effective is too demanding for the softness of the people? Isaiah says:

"It is a rebellious people that will not hear the law of the Lord, which say to the prophets, Prophesy not unto us *right things*, but speak unto us *smooth things* . . . get you out of the way, turn aside out of the path, cause the Holy One of Israel to cease from before us" (Isaiah 30:9-11).

How very human that is! The real prophet can never hope to be popular with very many people very long at a time. His message is too true and demanding, and it disturbs and hurts. When he speaks and it stings, one who is political-minded, fears *right things* that disturb and loves *smooth things* that please, says to his pastor, "That may be true, pastor, but ease off." The politic preacher can have it easy enough if he keeps to preaching the *smooth things,* studies the prejudices of his people, and deals in generalities and innocuous platitudes, and never opens new areas of truth that mean new responsibility. That was not Isaiah, nor was it Paul when he preached and when he counseled Timothy in the matter of his preaching, for Paul said:

"Preach the word. Be instant in season and out of season; reprove, rebuke, exhort, with all longsuffering and teaching" (II Timothy 4:2).

Is it a matter of personal and social justice? Isaiah says:

"I will make justice the line, and righteousness the plumet. . . . Then shall justice dwell in the wilderness; and righteousness shall abide in the fruitful field. And the work

62

of righteousness shall be peace, and the effect of righteousness, quietness and confidence forever. And my people shall dwell in a peaceful habitation, and in a safe dwelling, and in quiet dwelling places" (Isaiah 28:17 and Isaiah 32:16-18).

Is it a matter of the man who is truly good and great? Is it a matter of open-mindedness and open-handedness—truth, mercy, and generosity of life and behavior? Isaiah says:

"The vile person shall no more be called liberal, nor the churl said to be bountiful. . . . But the liberal deviseth liberal things; and by liberal things shall he stand" (Isaiah 32:5,8).

Is it a matter of hope and brightness ahead, when God is taken into the reckoning? Isaiah says:

"He hath made it glorious, Galilee of the nations. The people that walked in darkness have seen a great light; they that dwelt in the land of the shadow of death, upon them hath the light shined. . . . For unto us a child is born, unto us a son is given; and the government shall be upon his shoulders: and his name shall be called Wonderful, Counselor, Mighty God, the Everlasting Father, Prince of Peace. Of the increase of his government and peace there shall be no end. The zeal of the Lord of hosts will perform this" (Isaiah 9:2-7).

If we have done nothing else now than to hear these echoes from the sermons of this great outdoor preacher of Jerusalem—this man, who, if preaching today, would have a corner of Boston Common for his preaching place—we have not spent our time in vain. Hear these things and act upon them and your souls shall live.

Isaiah Was Very Sure of a Few Elemental and Foundational Things.

Isaiah was sure that he had been called of God to preach. When the splendid King Uzziah died, Isaiah was troubled.

He went off alone to the "temple." That temple may have been the actual temple of stone and timber in Jerusalem. That temple may have been a quiet spot amid a clump of trees in a garden near the very spot where Jesus later went to pray—Gethsemane. In either case Isaiah had a vision of God. It was a vision that never left him—never faded:

"I saw the Lord sitting upon a throne, high and lifted up, and his train filled the temple. Above him stood the seraphim: each one had six wings; with twain he covered his face; and with twain he covered his feet; and with twain he did fly. And one cried unto another and said, Holy, Holy, Holy is the Lord of hosts; the whole earth is full of his glory" (Isaiah 6:1-3).

Such a vision never was to fade. Even the seraphim before God covered their faces in reverence, their feet in humility, and spread one pair of wings to speed in God's service, to "post o'er land and ocean without rest." A preacher is sorely needed in Jerusalem. Isaiah knows that he is mortal and unclean, like other men. The live coal burns the iniquity from his lips, that is, the spirit of God cleanses his soul. Who will preach? Says Isaiah, "Here am I, send me." Isaiah never doubted his authority as a preacher. That authority was from God. Whether it be to the priests, to the king or to the people, Isaiah speaks the truth that comes from God, truth that hurts, but which, if obeyed, will heal. Paul had much in common with Isaiah in this matter of a clear and first-hand call from God. Thus, in the final chapter of the Acts of the Apostles, Paul reverted to Isaiah's temple vision, and added, "Be it known therefore unto you, that this salvation of God is sent unto the Gentiles" (Acts 28:28).

Isaiah was sure that the superstitions and sins of the leaders and the people were their own worst enemies. He denounced the empty formalism of the temple; he denounced the selfish injustice of the strong who preyed upon the weak. He saw sin as a violation of God, a violation of themselves,

64

and a violation of their fellow mortals in the city. "The people have not turned unto the Lord of hosts. Therefore the Lord will cut off from Israel head and tail, palm-branch and rush, in one day" (Isaiah 9:13-14).

Superstition and sin never pay in any coin but the wages of death. That was true of the life and behavior of Ahaz. There came a day when Ahaz was assailed by the Philistines and the Edomites. Isaiah continued to proclaim his gospel of faith in God. Ahaz, however, put his faith in horses and chariots. Ahaz had "broken faith badly with the Eternal" (Moffat). Ahaz sent for Tiglath-Pileser. The Assyrian came with an army. With one fist Tiglath-Pileser struck the Philistines and sent them reeling back home. With the other fist he struck the Edomites and sent them reeling back home. What did he do then? Did he go quietly back to Assyria? He did not. He marched very noisily to Jerusalem. In Jerusalem he assumed control. He took the gold and silver vessels from the temple. He robbed the king's own palace. He stripped the homes of the nobles. Thus did the chronicler say: "Tiglath-Pileser helped him not" (II Chronicles 28:21). Ahaz had broken faith badly with God. He forgot God so badly that he reverted to human sacrifice, after the fashion of the Baal worshipers. He offered his own children as human sacrifices in the flames. "He burnt his children in the fire" (II Chronicles 28:3). The sin of Ahaz was a violation of God, of himself and of other people. The price to be paid eventually was death to all possibility of peace and security and prosperity.

Isaiah was sure of the good will and the redeeming mercy of God. The condition upon which God could do His gracious work was the deep and genuine repentance of the people. "In returning and rest ye shall be saved; in quietness and in confidence shall be your strength" (Isaiah 30:15). That means genuine repentance—an about turn in their whole thought, outlook, and behavior. That would give God a chance to change and redeem them. "Ye turn things upside down! Shall the potter be esteemed as the clay; that the thing made should say of him that made it, He made me not? or the thing formed say of him that formed it, He hath no understanding?" (Isaiah 29:16). Isaiah is calling, pleading, appealing to the people to give God a chance at them, to let the Divine Potter mold again the human clay. God can change them and He can change and save the city, if they will but repent. Yes, God can change our modern humanity and save the world if we will give Him a chance.

There is an old story which comes from Scotland, the story of Fairy Loch. Fairy Loch is a little lake in the hills at Tarbot, not far from Loch Lomond. The quality of the rock at the bottom of Fairy Loch is such that when one looks down into the water, he sees a mixture of colors. The legend of Fairy Loch tells that once that spot was the abode of the fairies. The work of these fairies was to dye the cloth for the people of that highland area. The men would carry their bundles of wool and cloth and leave them near the loch. Beside each bundle was also left a piece of yarn of the color to which the wool or cloth was to be dyed. In the night the fairies did their work. In the morning the newly-dyed bundles of wool and cloth were taken away. One night a highlander left beside Fairy Loch the fleece of a black sheep. Beside the fleece of the black sheep he left a piece of white yarn. He wanted the black fleece changed into white. That night the fairies came to their work as usual. When they saw the black fleece which was to be changed into white, they were dismayed. They could change white into gray, gray into brown, or brown into black. But to change black into white was utterly beyond them. They threw all their dyes into the loch and left the place forever. In legend that accounts for the colors at the bottom of Fairy Loch. In that legend is a deep spiritual truth. We can and we have changed white into black, but our pretty superstitions—the fairies—

66

cannot change the black back to white again. Isaiah knew that. Thus toward the end of his mighty ministry, he said:

"Come now, let us bring our reasoning to a close. Though your sins be as scarlet, they shall be white as snow; though they be red like crimson, they shall be as wool" (Isaiah 1:18).

The grace of God can do it. Then

"A king shall reign in righteousness, and princes shall rule in justice. A man shall be as a hiding place from the wind, and a covert from the tempest, as rivers in a dry place, as the shadow of a great rock in a weary land. And the eyes of them that see shall not be dim and the ears of them that hear shall hearken" (Isaiah 32:1-3).

Isaiah, across the centuries we hear thy voice, courageous and clear. It calls upon us to repent. Today we respond. Isaiah, thou of the bright foregleams of the incarnate mercy and of a redeemed humanity, we hearken. Isaiah, it is true that "unto us the child has been born, unto us the Son has been given. Jesus is here. He is the realization of thy brightest vision, the fulfilment of thy grandest hope. We listen, as we are called upon to listen. We repent, as we must repent. We trust, for in Him our trust is well placed. We follow, for in Him there is life that is right and peaceful and satisfying.

"Come, ye disconsolate, where'er ye languish;
Come to the Mercy Seat, fervently kneel;
Here bring your wounded hearts;
Here tell your anguish;
Earth has no sorrow that heaven cannot heal."

VIII

NEHEMIAH

The Decision To Rebuild

"So we built the wall . . . unto half thereof."—NEHE-
MIAH 4:6.
"So the wall was finished."—NEHEMIAH 6:15.

THE condition which demanded the work of Nehemiah was
not a sudden happening, but rather the consummation of
processes which had gone on for many generations in and
about Jerusalem.

In the story of Nehemiah at Jerusalem we find the people
of Judah and the Samaritans in open clash with each other.
That is new. The Samaritans have become a self-conscious
group, different from either Israel or Judah. Sargon II of
Assyria had attacked Samaria and had taken away some
27,000 nobles. These men were scattered in Assyrian terri-
tory and they had disappeared permanently. There was no
return from exile for them. II Kings 17:24 says, "The king
of Assyria brought men from Babylon, and from Cuthah,
and from Avva, and from Hamath and Sepharvaim, and
placed them in cities of Samaria instead of the children of
Israel; and they possessed Samaria and dwelt in the cities
thereof." By the time of Nehemiah the mixed people of
Samaria had become known as Samaritans and there was a
spirit of fierce enmity between them and the people of
Judah, especially of Jerusalem. In the days of Jesus that
enmity still existed. Today a group of some one hundred
and fifty Samaritans perpetuate the traditions of their distinct group. Nehemiah met that condition.

Nehemiah also met the condition of a Jerusalem reduced
to ruins by two Babylonian invasions and by the plundering
of near-by groups. Nebuchadnezzar took away some ten

thousand in the "first captivity." In the "second captivity" all the others who seemed worth taking away were transported to Babylonia. Those remaining were a dispirited and disorganized and helpless group. The Jews of the first and second captivity had been in Babylonia for fifty years when Cyrus the Persian conquered Babylon. Cyrus is of generous nature and proclaims liberation for the Jews if they wish to go home. Some did go. Many others remained in the Tigris-Euphrates valley to enjoy their prosperity in business and the temporal delights of the city of Babylon, with its gorgeous hanging gardens and its endless opportunity for pleasure.

No modern city, with its night-club life, has outdone Babylon in what it had to offer in entertainment. It would have been as difficult to convince many thousands of prosperous Jews in Babylonia that they should return to Jerusalem as it would be now to convince many prosperous Jews in New York that they should move to Palestine. Prosperous Jews in Babylon entered the gay life of the city until the great unknown preacher of the exile, whose messages appear in Isaiah 40 to 55, said "Wherefore do ye spend your money for that which is not bread? and your labor for that which satisfieth not? hearken diligently unto me, and eat ye that which is good, and let your soul delight itself in fatness. Incline your ear unto me; hear and your soul shall live" (Isaiah 55:2-3). Some of those who remained and zealously organized in groups for study, discipline and worship, which resulted in the synagogue, may have shared the vision of the great unknown preacher, stated in the Songs of the Suffering Servant, that the purpose of God for His people in their captivity was that they should be missionaries to Babylon and the world beyond Babylon.

Back in Jerusalem, Zerubbabel had rebuilt the temple. The walls of the city, however, are in ruins. The people are broken in spirit. There is nobody to lead them. Hanani, a brother of Nehemiah, comes to Babylon and relates the sad story of Jerusalem's plight to Nehemiah.

This condition, briefly stated, was not a sudden thing, but the consummation of a process of deterioration that had been going on for generations.

Nehemiah decides that he will do something about Jerusalem. He will be a rebuilder. His decision has everything to do with his destiny and the destiny of a nation.

Nehemiah, Who Proposed to Be a Rebuilder, Had Succeeded in Building Himself into a Strong and Worthy Person. To read the observations and interpretations of Nehemiah is to meet with a very intelligent man. He saw more than met the eye. He saw meanings in conditions and events. Nehemiah was a dependable man. That is why he had been exalted to the position of cupbearer to Artaxerxes, the king. Like any other despot, Artaxerxes had to be constantly on guard against attempts to take his life. Poison might be dropped into the wine goblet of the autocrat. Nehemiah watched against that and tasted of the king's cup before handing it to him. He was likely one of a group of cupbearers, who were the king's personal bodyguards. Nehemiah was a careful planner. When he actually set out on his adventure to Jerusalem, he was accompanied by a detachment of cavalry and he carried letters of authority from Artaxerxes. Those letters gave him authority to cut timber from the royal domains and they were his credentials of authority at Jerusalem. Nehemiah was a brave man. Adverse conditions did not deter him. He was a good leader and executive, as his organization of work at Jerusalem demonstrates. Above all, he was a zealous, religious patriot, narrowed by an intense racialism that we consider foreign to the Christian spirit, but unselfishly devoted to his people and to Jerusalem.

Such is the man who is sad in the presence of Artaxerxes. Such is the man who dares to ask the king for a commission to do nothing less than go to Jerusalem and rebuild the broken walls of the city.

When Nehemiah arrived at Jerusalem he did what any wise man would do—he made a careful survey of the ruined walls, of the fallen gates, and, above all, of the spirit of the people.

Nehemiah Saw that the Central Cause of the People's Distress Was Their Own Sin. If tragedy had approached the people from without, it was just as true that they had been weakened to the point of being victims by the sin that ravaged them from within.

A few lines of failure constantly left the people open to tragedy. They had a habit of reverting to idols. The strong among them preyed upon the weak. Nehemiah had to correct that condition. Mortgages had resulted in the sons and daughters of some Jews becoming the slaves of others. That Nehemiah corrected. The people had the weakness of our day; they turned the day of worship into a day of profit-making business and riotous pleasure.

Sin is a violation of self, a violation of others, and a violation of God. Nehemiah saw that as the central problem in the whole tragic picture. Thus he prays, "I confess the sins of the children of Israel, which we have sinned against thee. Yea, I and my father's house have sinned; we have dealt very corruptly against thee, and have not kept the commandments." Nehemiah did not hold himself aloof or above the others. He included himself among the sinners.

Sin offers delights, but sin deceives. Then sin deteriorates. At last sin destroys. Nehemiah saw that that was the central problem of Jerusalem. It is the central problem of our tragedy-ridden world. To defeat Hitler and his evil-purposed combination of enslavers is necessary. To defeat sin in all our hearts is the deeper and more central battle. It is the great personal and global war.

The Rebuilding of Nehemiah Was Designed to Give the

*People the Opportunity of Life that Was Peaceful, Digni-
fied, Righteous and Worthy.* Thus the great rebuilder sets
to work at Jerusalem. The wall is to protect the people from
military attack. His plan of organizing his workers is interesting in its comprehensiveness. There is no statement that
carpenters or masons were available, but priests and gold-
smiths and apothecaries became amateur masons. The
priests work opposite the area of the temple. The plan involved men working opposite their own houses. If in the
enterprise of the kingdom we build that section of the wall
opposite to our own lives and churches we are following an
efficient and comprehensive plan. To the disgrace of one
group it is said, "The Tekoites repaired; but their nobles
put not their necks to the work of the Lord."

Nehemiah had great opposition. He was opposed by San-
ballat and his Samaritans and the groups who gathered
around the Samaritans. These threatened military attack.
He had the broken spirits of the people with which to contend. At one point they were very sure that they could not
continue, and they said, "We are not able to build the wall"
(Nehemiah 4:10). He had to deal with treachery. She-
maiah attempted to have Nehemiah take refuge in the
temple as a place of protection against those who would kill
him. To that proposal he replied, "Who is there, that being
such as I, would go into the temple to save his life? I will
not go in." It was, as Nehemiah saw, a plot to discredit him
as a coward. Above all, he had to contend with the rumor
mongers. Whenever any man or woman shows initiative
enough to do a worth-while deed and build a worth-while
wall, there is always the person with the evil mind and the
slanderous tongue. Thus Gashmu appears and Nehemiah
received through his servant a letter, reading, "It is reported
among the nations, and Gashmu saith it, that thou and the
Jews think to rebel, for which cause thou art building the
wall, and thou wouldest be their king, according to these

words [these rumors]. And thou hast also appointed prophets to preach of thee at Jerusalem, saying, There is a king in Judah: and now it shall be reported to the king [Artaxerxes] according to these words." Nehemiah made short work of that rumor. He merely complimented his enemies on having such imaginations that they would create such rumors out of their own hearts. He went on with his work, praying, "O God, strengthen thou my hands" (Nehemiah 6:6-9).

Nehemiah, moreover, would protect the people from each other. He had seen the evil of one strong man taking advantage of weaker Jews and enslaving them. He fostered that spirit of brotherhood that would give justice to all.

Above all, Nehemiah saw that if the people were to be strong and free and live in dignified peace, they must take God into the reckoning. Worship must be real and their allegiance to the laws of God must be genuine. He saw that there was a living relationship between experiencing the mercies of God and being true to God. Thus he says, "Walk in the fear of God," and "Stand up and bless the Lord your God." Reverent worship and the loyal heart would make the individual and the nation strong.

We are now engaged not only in a great war to destroy a destroyer, but in an enterprise of building and rebuilding a home for God's redeemed humanity. In the *Kiwanis Service Club Magazine* of September, 1939, appeared these lines:

> "I watched them tearing a building down,
> A gang of men in a busy town.
> With a ho-heave-ho and a lusty yell
> They swung a beam and a side wall fell.

> "I asked the foreman, 'Are these men skilled
> As the men you'd hire if you had to build?'
> He gave a laugh and said, 'No, indeed!
> Just common labor is all I need.
> I can easily wreck in a day or two
> What builders have taken a year to do.'

> "I thought to myself as I went my way,
>   'Which of these rules have I tried to play?
>   Am I a builder who works with care
>   Measuring life by the rule and square?
>   Am I shaping my deeds to a well-laid plan,
>   Patiently doing the best I can?
>   Or am I a wrecker who walks the town
>   Content with the labor of tearing down?' " *

When General Douglas MacArthur was a young man he was director of athletics at the U. S. Military Academy. Over the door of the gymnasium leading to the stadium he placed these words: "On this field are sown the seeds of future victories." These young men are now away fighting the battle for America and human freedom. "Sowing seeds" is merely changing the metaphor from building to planting. In the practice of worship of and loyalty to God, as we know Him in Jesus Christ, we are building builders. Jesus said, "Every one therefore which heareth these words of mine, and doeth them, shall be likened unto a wise man, which built his house upon the rock: and the rain descended, and the floods came, and the winds blew, and beat upon that house; and it fell not: for it was founded upon the rock" (Matthew 7:24-25).

* Used by permission of the Editor.

IX

DANIEL

The Decision For Religious Liberty

"And when Daniel knew that the writing was signed, he went into his house (now his windows were open in his chamber toward Jerusalem); and he kneeled upon his knees three times a day, and prayed, and gave thanks before his God, as he did aforetime."—DANIEL 6:10.

THAT was a daring declaration of religious liberty. In the midst of a pagan despotism that held the threat of death over him for his nonconformity, this zealous Jew worshiped God according to his own conscience. It is a beautiful touch, telling of religious patriotism and fearless faith, which has portrayed Daniel going to his oratory of prayer—his chamber—with "his windows open toward Jerusalem." This story of Daniel was told and retold by some flaming unknown preacher in a day when again the Hebrew nation was faced with a "fiery furnace" and a "den of lions." It was told to engender courage and to keep the people true to their God.

The time of the preaching summarized in Daniel is in the middle of the second century, B.C., from 175 to 163 B.C. Antiochus Epiphanes of Syria, more accurately known as Antiochus The Mad, rather than Antiochus The Brilliant, was determined to promote Greek culture and religion at Jerusalem and throughout Judea. He had gone by military force into Jerusalem. At the temple he had destroyed the altar of the true God and had erected an altar to the Greek Zeus. On that altar pagan priests, not in the spirit of worship, but going out of their way to offend Jerusalem, offered swine as a sacrifice (I Maccabees 1:41-64). When we remember the Jewish feeling toward swine, we can partly understand the depth and the cruelty of the insult thrown into their faces. Nothing could be quite so horrible as that in the eyes of the devout Jew—swine offered to Zeus as a sacrifice on a pagan altar at the temple of the Lord. That was the "abomination of desolation" referred to in Daniel 11:31 and 12:11.

That abominable thing was not accepted in cowardly silence or supine inaction by the Jews. Up among the hills of Judah lived an aged priest, Mattathias of Modin. He defiantly refused to offer swine's flesh as a burnt offering. Indeed, he went further than that. He struck and killed a faithless and renegade Jew who had gone apostate so far as to conform to the demands of the soldiers and priests of Antiochus.

At that point emerges Judas Maccabæus, whose story is preserved in the apocryphal books of the Maccabees, books so full of interest for the student of Bible history, but books removed from our Bible partly by the hand of Martin Luther. The name Judas Maccabæus means "Judas the Hammerer." He struck hard against the enemies of the Temple and the people's God. It would be difficult to match him among daring, courageous and successful military leaders. He repeatedly defeated the Syrians in combat where the mathematics of warfare said he was defeated before the battles began. But with a smaller army made up of "Ironsides" he hammered out victory after victory, and entered Jerusalem.

In Jerusalem on December 25, 105 B.C., Judas Maccabæus tore down and destroyed the altar of Zeus, cleansed the temple and rebuilt an altar to God. The ancient sacrifices were again offered. A great Feast of Dedication was held, the feast which we see Jesus attending in the story given by the writer of the Gospel of John (John 10:22. Also I Maccabees 4:52-59). That feast was regularly celebrated by the Jews on the 25th of December, and it continued for eight days. The success of the fighting religious patriots under Judas

76

Maccabæus was so emphatic that in 103 B.C. the Syrian king granted religious liberty to the Jews.

That is the historic scene in which some unknown preacher in Judea encouraged the people to fight on by retelling an old story of a courageous Jew, Daniel, in Babylon, some three centuries before. Fiery furnaces and dens of lions did not silence Daniel. Neither would the fierceness of the Syrian Antiochus subdue the people of Judea and Jerusalem in that fierce period in the middle of the second century B.C.

It was as though in Bohemia, Czecho Slovakia, the soldiers of Adolf Hitler took over a church where the name of John Huss was honored. Imagine that in that church the Nazis erected a Nazi altar in honor of Nazism and placed on it *Mein Kampf.* Then Bohemian patriots led by some fiery religious patriot defeated the Nazi oppressor, cleared out the church and restored the worship of God in the church. Such a thing—which may yet happen—would be a modern parallel to the work of Judas Maccabæus at the temple of Jerusalem.

The literary cast of the book of Daniel is well known in the time period to which it belongs. If an unknown, obscure man who had something important to say, wished his message to be heard, would he give that message in the name of some ancient worthy, some name which held the admiring attention of people.

Indeed, one of the very effective "Victory Books" of England today, entitled *Guilty Men,* which has gone through more than twenty editions to more than 125,000 copies, bears "Cato" as the name of the author. Cato was the ancient Roman statesman and patriot who spoke and struggled against Hannibal and Hasdrubal and was the originator of the phrase *Delenda est Carthago*—"Carthage must be destroyed." It is an interesting thing that even a modern author who wishes quick and effective attention should revert to an old literary custom and send his book out under the name of an ancient statesman—Cato.

77

Thus the unknown preacher who supports the military endeavors of Judas Maccabæus strengthens patriotism, religion, and morale by speaking in the name of an ancient worthy, Daniel. Beyond that, he tells the story as if it were at the actual time of its happening, some three hundred years previous. The courageous Jew in the story is in action in 598 B.C., in Babylon. The preacher, who is Judas Maccabæus' chief chaplain and morale builder, writes and speaks during the campaign of Judas, from 168 to 164 B.C.

Then it must be remembered that the story of Daniel and his companions has been told and retold in Jewish homes for three centuries. They are stories not reduced to writing, but told from generation to generation. Those stories do not grow less with time. Indeed, in a century and a half legends of George Washington have been rounded out, even with written records to moderate the process. In far less than three-quarters of a century, with written records to check by, legends of Abraham Lincoln have grown up which would surprise him. What does it matter if three centuries of telling about Daniel meant the growth of a great story from the simple foundation of a courageous Jew who refused to conform to Babylonian paganism, no matter what punishments were inflicted?

As the unknown preacher of the book of Daniel comes nearer to his own age his history becomes very accurate. Then he makes a slip in his record which is the key for scholars to fix the date at which at least a portion of the book was written. The author is deeply resentful of Antiochus. After such arrogant and insulting behavior Antiochus should die a disgraceful death in one of his military adventures. In Daniel 11:40-45 the author consigns Antiochus to the sort of death he should die in the sort of place where that death should take place. He says, "He shall go forth with great fury to destroy and utterly to sweep away many. And he shall plant the tents of his palace between the sea and the glorious mountain; yet he shall come to his end, and none shall come to his aid, and none shall help him." It is pointed out by scholars that the author of Daniel, venturing into predictions, goes wrong at this point.

Professor I. G. Matthews writes:

"No doubt there were evidences that Antiochus was gathering a force by which he might avenge himself on the Egyptians (Daniel 11:40-43), but affairs in the East attracted him, and history knows of no attack on Egypt after 168 B.C. No doubt it would have been the correct thing in a world of law and order that Antiochus should have set up his tent between the 'sea and the glorious mountain,' and that there, the center of his infamy, he 'should come to his end.' Historical facts do not always follow the pathway of theocratic justice, and in this case we know that the culprit died in Tabae in the land of Persia (I Maccabees 6:5-17)." *

Professor Frederick Carl Eiselen writes: "The book of Daniel in its present form originated in the days of Antiochus Epiphanes (175-163 B.C.); in other words it was the outgrowth of the Maccabean troubles, and was intended to comfort and inspire the oppressed Jewish believers of that age." ** When we approach the book of Daniel with that understanding of it, it is a glowing series of religiously patriotic sermons. They strengthened the Jews of that fierce and dark day and they strengthen us when once again the fiery furnace and the lions are threats to the lovers of God and of liberty. Such an understanding of the book of Daniel also saves us from the repeated absurdities of those who have attempted to use it as one would use a New York Central Railway time-table, to give stations and times ahead. Daniel was never given to us to tell when Hitler will fall or when Russia will come to her end, or when Britain or America

 * From *Old Testament Life and Literature,* p. 305. Used by permission of The Macmillan Company, publishers, New York City.
  ** From *Prophecy and the Prophets,* p. 301. By permission of The Methodist Book Concern, publishers, New York.

will crumble. Such use of the Book of Daniel is a travesty on the Christian faith and leaves the followers of it open to inevitable disappointment. The message of the book of Daniel is one of faith and loyalty in the face of oppression and the determination to be free in worship and life as the free-born sons of God. As such it is a flaming and heartening message from the soul of a mighty preacher. As such we need it now and are grateful for it.

Daniel refused to be subdued by the threat of the lions' den. He continued to open his windows toward Jerusalem and pray. God did not forsake him. We too can be free if we live by faith in God and loyalty to our natures as sons of God.

The story of the Christian fellowship is the story of freedom. For freedom men and women have endured hardness and accepted death. The death of Christian martyrs has always forwarded the cause of liberty rather than defeated it. You cannot kill truth and a cause by murdering a leader. Rather the truth and the cause will prosper.

The epic of Christianity is the picture of Jerusalem, Rome, London, and Boston, where heroic souls have chosen death instead of suppression and by their free spirits set the future free. Now that liberty is challenged again by a modern pagan despotism, the free sons of God have risen and put their armor on. Christian men will fight through, they will "stand fast in the liberty wherewith Christ hath made us free," and refuse to be enslaved again by any "yoke of bondage." "Brethren, ye are called unto liberty."

X

MATTHEW

The Decision To Change Work

> "And it came to pass, as he sat at meat in the house, behold, many publicans and sinners sat down with Jesus and his disciples."—MATTHEW 9:10.

MATTHEW the publican gave a dinner party with Jesus as the guest of honor. There were present at that dinner party a group of Jesus' disciples and "many publicans." What a target for the arrows of criticism from the bows of Jesus' enemies, the Pharisees. They did not miss the opportunity to shoot those arrows without delay.

This feast of Matthew tells the story of a man who had made an important change in his life plan—a change of work. Work for the purposeful man becomes his other self, or it is himself, his very life. Such a decision has everything to do with the destiny of the man himself and the destiny of those whom his life and work touch.

A Feast of Resignation. This feast of Matthew was a feast of resignation. He was leaving an old post of work forever. Many another person has been a guest of honor at the completion of a long term of work. When he resigned, his friends gave him a dinner party and spoke freely of what he had been and done in his vocation. This dinner party, however, was different. It was given, not by a man at the end of his working years, but by a man who was comparatively young and who had vigor and ability. He was leaving a post of work of which he had become ashamed. The dinner party announced that he had resigned from his post under Cæsar to accept a position with a homeless carpenter. This dinner party, moreover, was not given to Matthew by his friends, but rather it was planned by Matthew and given at his own expense.

81

The work of the publican was at once gainful and disgraceful. Rome "farmed out" the business of collecting taxes and customs. The holder of the post of publican, in modern speech, was a "Quisling." A publican was a Jew who sold out to Rome. He was given the right to collect taxes from his fellow Jews in a given area at a contract price. When he paid that price, all the additional money he had collected became his personal profit. The position was enormously profitable and deeply disgraceful. A man like Matthew sold out his place in the community; he lost his friends. He sold out his place at the synagogue; he was not a brother, but an oppressor. He sold out his place as a citizen; patriotism was dead. Matthew was living in ostracized prosperity.

This feast announced that Matthew had resigned his post with the government of Rome. He was making money, but he was losing everything else that made life worth while.

Matthew very likely had heard Jesus more than a few times before he stepped out of his toll booth beside the highway that led around the head of the Lake of Galilee. Very likely he had talked with Jesus. Back in the toll booth, when he had taken an exorbitant amount as custom duty for a traveling merchant, he heard echoes of Jesus remark, "Ye cannot serve God and mammon." Like Belshazzar at his feast, a sentence appeared, as though on a wall, "You cannot serve God and mammon." Conscience kept repeating it. And at last conscience and the call of Jesus won out in the soul of Matthew and he resigned, stepped out of the post given him by Cæsar, for he was ashamed of what he had been and what he had done. This feast was the announcement that he was through with that forever. Moreover, he was saying that to fellow publicans who were at the dinner party.

It is significant that when Matthew, Mark, and Luke give the list of the apostles Mark and Luke merely give the name "Matthew," but when Matthew himself gives the list, he writes it, "Matthew the publican." Matthew thus openly confessed his own unworthy behavior. He is ashamed of it, breaks clear of it all—resigns. That is one of the meanings of the dinner party.

A Feast of Declaration. On the positive side, the feast of Matthew was a feast of open declaration. He declares himself openly for Jesus.

That meant a great deal. It meant leaving financial security for financial insecurity. Said Jesus, "The foxes have holes and the birds of the air have nests, but the Son of man hath not where to lay his head." That is a supreme test.

"The love of money is a root of all kinds of evil." Very often that is misquoted, and Paul is made to say, "Money is the root of all evil." Money is necessary. It is a symbol of value by which we buy and sell. When the love of that symbol rules in the soul all sorts of evil follow. Matthew was making the declaration that the center of his loyalty was henceforth not his love for money, but his love for Jesus Christ.

Everything in life turns on what is the center of our deepest affections. It was a great Scottish preacher, Thomas Chalmers, who put that truth in immortal phrase when he spoke of "the expulsive power of a new affection." That new center of affection, however, is more than "expulsive." It does more than expel the publican spirit from men. It is creative. It is everything Jesus meant by "the new birth." When Jesus is the center of a man's deepest affections it means a new understanding of and a new attitude toward God. It means a new attitude toward self. The man lives with a new ideal ever before him. It means a new attitude toward people. Indeed, Jesus went the distance of saying, "By this shall all men know that ye are my disciples, if ye have love the one to the other."

That feast, as Dr. A. B. Bruce has put it in *The Training*

of the Twelve, was Matthew, saying what Doddridge said
in his universally known gospel song,

> "O happy day, that fixed my choice
> On Thee, my Saviour, and my God!

> "Well may this glowing heart rejoice
> And tell its raptures all abroad.

> " 'Tis done, the great transaction's done:
> I am my Lord's and He is mine.

> "He drew me, and I followed on,
> Charmed to confess the voice divine."

A Feast of Introduction. The feast of Matthew was a
feast of introduction. Matthew was introducing his fellow
publicans to Jesus. Some of them may have met Jesus before. Some of them may have heard Him. Now they could
ask Him questions and hear Him answer.

Whom did they meet and what did they meet when Matthew introduced his fellow publicans to Jesus?

Matthew was introducing these publicans to the One who
was the answer to the great question of the soul. In Jesus
is the answer to the question, "What is God like?" for He
said, "He who hath seen me hath seen the Father." In Jesus
was the answer to the question, "What is the meaning of
life?" His own life is that answer. It is to know our natures
as His kinsmen and sons of God, and to seek life in the plane
appropriate to sons of God.

In Jesus they found the answer to the sin question. Sin is
a violation of God, of ourselves and of others that is deadly.
Jesus is the Deliverer and Redeemer. He was criticized by
the Pharisees for being among publicans and sinners. His
answer was, "They that be whole need not a physician, but
they that are sick." Jesus granted to that pharisaic criticism
their own healthy condition—that was a masterly thrust at
their pharisaic hypocrisy—but said that His concern was for

the "sick." He, the Great Physician, was the answer to sin. He forgave, He cleansed, He remade.

In Jesus, these publicans had the answer to the question about life's responsibility. Even to keep away from sin is not enough. Life is real when it spends itself in sacrificial and redemptive endeavor. In Jesus these publicans had the answer to the question about human destiny. He was to walk through death to life. His own statement was, "I am the resurrection and the life. He that believeth in me, though he were dead yet shall he live."

The person whom Matthew introduced to his fellow publicans—Jesus—was God's answer to the deep, demanding question of the soul about God, sin, the meaning of life, responsibility, and destiny.

Surely Matthew's feast is a picture of concern for others and a desire to share a great good thing that must forever stand as a thrilling example to the Church, whose business it is to introduce the people of earth to her Lord. What an answer He is to our present need for a leader who will open the way to human life and liberty.

A Feast of Dedication. The feast of Matthew was a feast of dedication. Matthew was henceforth out and out for Jesus and the Kingdom of God.

Dr. Alexander Whyte of Edinburgh once said that the only things that Matthew took with him from the toll booth were his pen and ink. The suggestion is that he used them in writing a book. Back in the days of slavery, when people were feeling keenly about that great evil, a sister of Harriet Beecher Stowe wrote to her and said, "Hattie, if I could use my pen as you can yours, I would write something that would stir this nation." Harriet Beecher Stowe responded. She responded in *Uncle Tom's Cabin.* Later, when Abraham Lincoln met Harriet Beecher Stowe, he said, "So you are the little lady who made the Civil War." Abraham Lincoln was stating that the cause of human liberty had been advanced by the use of a consecrated pen. Scholars doubtless are right that other hands than Matthew's did some of the writing that has found its way into the gospel that bears his name. The main story, however, is as Matthew wrote it. It was Matthew who preserved one of the beautiful nativity stories and the great summary of Jesus' preaching, the Sermon on the Mount. As long as men read anything they will be reading what was left in a book by this man Matthew, who consecrated to God his "pen and ink."

There is little else told us about Matthew beyond the fact that Jesus called him from the toll booth and that Matthew followed; that he gave a feast at which Jesus and some of His disciples and many publicans were present; and that we have a gospel of which he was the writer. Within that, however, is the record of a man who met Jesus and because of that changed his work. That has happened with great souls like D. L. Moody and Albert Schweitzer.

As you meet Jesus today it may mean a major change of work for you. Or it may mean a new consecration of what you are already about. At any rate, it means that Jesus has called and you have risen in your place, stepped out into a new life and that you are going to follow.

Oh, for the courage of Douglas who, in his fight with the Moors in Spain, flung the silver-casketed heart of Bruce into the thickest of the fight and then said, "O heart of Bruce, I'll follow thee or die." He did. Let us plant the white banner of Jesus before us in a sinful and tragedy-ridden world, and say, "O Jesus Christ, I'll follow Thee till I die!"

XI

PETER

The Decision To Change Masters

"Then answered Peter and said unto him, We have left all and followed thee; what shall we have therefore?"— MATTHEW 19:27.

YOU have often looked at reproductions of that striking painting by Hofmann, "The Great Refusal." It shows Jesus in conversation with a handsome, richly-robed young Jew. Jesus is appealing to him for his companionship and his help. The hands of Jesus are outstretched in the appeal, but the young man is turning on his heel to go away. Jesus had required that the rich young ruler give up his wealth, and he could not do it. He went away sorrowful, for he had great possessions.

When the disciples of Jesus saw that splendid, intelligent young man turn away, they began to ask questions. They compared his action with their own. At least, some of them were not altogether poor, for they had a fishing business of considerable proportions at the head of the Lake of Galilee. Peter, the ready and forthright spokesman of the rest, expressed the feelings and thinking of the group. The remark of Peter was thoroughly in accord with his open-souled honesty when he said, "Lo, we have left all and followed thee; what shall we have therefore?"

Peter and his companions wondered whether they had made a major mistake. If a splendid, intelligent person like this rich young ruler had decided against the proposal of Jesus, had they blundered? Were they following a visionary idealist in a forlorn hope? The answer of Jesus is, "Verily I say unto you, That ye which have followed me, in the regeneration when the Son of man shall sit on the throne of his glory, ye also shall sit upon twelve thrones, judging the twelve tribes of Israel." Jesus is asking His men to take the long view at life.

The question of Peter raises two other important questions.

What Are The Rewards Which Men Seek In Life? William I. Thomas, in his book, *The Unadjusted Girl,** has made a study of the dominant desires of people, the rewards which they wish to win. May we match these desires against our own and see whether he has not identified things which we all wish.

The first great desire which is identified is the desire for new experience. It is the hankering for adventure into the unexplored and the unknown. When a young lad at home pelts his father with questions about the sun and the moon and about God—questions which are at once the pride and despair of parents—what else is it but that young mind feeling out into the unknown? I can distinctly remember a pair of young boys, whose home was beside a lake, in an adventure for new experience. One day they were off swimming with the other lads. Then on making their way home they crossed a railway track. The older boy, eleven years old, remembered that at the next village along that single track railway an uncle lived. He had often wondered what it was like in the unknown world west beyond the curve in the railway. They started away and rounded the curve. They kept on walking, two barefoot boys, one eleven and one nine years of age, over the cinder bed of the railway. They rounded many curves. The darkness came, but they walked on. At nine o'clock that night, tired out, they arrived, nine miles away, at the village and the home of their uncle. The uncle and aunt fed them and put them off to bed. Then they telephoned to the boys' home to tell the terrified par-

* *The Unadjusted Girl,* p. 4. Used by permission of the publishers, Little, Brown and Company, Boston.

ents, who had decided that the boys had been drowned, that they were safe in bed and sound asleep. I know all about that walk, for I was that older boy. Moreover, that curve in life's road is still there. Life keeps beckoning on and one wants to know what it is like out beyond that next curve. It is the magnetic pull of adventure into the new and the hitherto unknown.

Another desire, as stated by William I. Thomas, is the desire for security. People want to be secure from want and suffering. They seek that by gaining an amount of wealth. That is why insurance policies sell and that is why we build up bank accounts. That is why now national leaders like Mr. Roosevelt and Mr. Churchill write Atlantic charters and plans for international councils. Security is one of the rewards we wish to gain in life.

Again, there is the desire for recognition. Some men are content to be utterly obscure. Most men, however, want to be recognized as worth-while people doing a worth-while thing. Give a boy a jackknife, and before long he will be found carving his initials on a barn wall or a fence post or a tree. That desire is strong in the human heart.

Further, there is the desire for response. There are men who are "lone birds," who are content to live as hermits. But such men are marked men and are considered as departing from the normal ways of life. Lately I heard a person stating a plan to go away for a rest. A quiet spot by the sea was suggested. At once the answer came, "But there would be nobody there now. I would be utterly alone and I do not want that." People naturally wish the delights of friendships—the response of other lives. That desire is seen —and it is realized—when two young lives gravitate toward each other and a marriage is consummated and a new home is established.

Surely, in these four dominant desires for new experience, security, recognition and response, we have been rather well understood by Mr. William I. Thomas. One of the tragic facts of life, however, is that when these things are sought in the wrong way, the desires are never realized and life is dull, insecure, obscure and lonely.

What Are the Best Rewards of Life? I dare to think that when Peter decided upon Jesus as a Master and adventured with this purpose, he was doing something which brought rewards which included all that is best in these dominant desires at which we have looked.

"What shall we have therefore?" asked honest-souled Peter.

Here are the things which are won in the adventure with Jesus:

Progress In Personal Culture. There is progress in personal culture. Jesus uttered a most important fact of life for His men when He said, "Follow me and I will make you . . ." He does make men. No man can live in His fellowship and share in His purposeful endeavors without himself growing into a better person. I recall Dr. J. H. Jowett telling that at sixty years of age he placed himself under the direction of a teacher to learn sketching. At first he practiced drawing certain simple lines freehand. A little later he worked at certain curves. One day he was allowed to do some simple sketching. Dr. Jowett was sixty years of age, but he was still busy at drawing forth one more power from a life that seemed to be so beautifully developed already. Such a man builds a world of personality which can never be taken from him. Jesus does that with men. He makes them as they practice the art of life with Him.

Take the matter of moral liberty. Nobody can give us liberty. It must be won. Liberty is the power and the will to be and do what we ought to be and do at each turn of life. Thus it is a product of a lifelong endeavor. Liberty is not rebellion against law. It is knowing law and living by it until liberty is known in law. That is true in the matter of physical health. It is a matter of knowing the laws of health and living by them. That way lies freedom from disease, or, at least, the best possibility for freedom from disease. That is true of the correct and elegant use of English. Formal grammar is thought to be a slow and cumbersome thing. But when the laws of grammar are known, then the student uses English with correctness, ease, and effectiveness. He naturally speaks and writes correctly. That is true of music. A child works hour after hour at the scales—week after week and month after month. Then one day a young pianist plays a beautiful selection with a touch and a rhythm that delights both herself and her friends. That is true in life. There are great laws of life which should be known. Jesus announced them in the Beatitudes. When these are known and worked at, as though in a gymnasium of life, then character attains that freedom whereby at each turn of the road we at least approximate being and doing what we ought to be and do. That is achieved when Jesus is really Master.

What about the commendation of one's own conscience? There is an inner citadel of life where at times we are utterly alone. Then, when I say to myself something about the behavior of yesterday, is it a condemnation or a commendation? What peace and assurance were the possessions of the great apostle when he could say, "I have fought a good fight; I have finished my course; I have kept the faith." Nobody can give to another a commendation of conscience. It must be won. It can be won when Jesus is Master.

Think of the matter of the confidence of those who know us best. Reputations are what the world has given us. They may be false or true. But to know that we live in the love and confidence of those who know us best—that is a reward worth gaining. I once heard grand old Dr. John Clifford say, "I live in the love of my friends." He was then a man over eighty years of age. That was a reward of lifelong integrity and generosity.

Surely a crowning reward of life under the Mastery of Jesus is the sense that a man has lived usefully. That usefulness may never be recognized in a biography or a monument. A far better thing is what you have built into other lives.

All this was realized by Peter at last. The rich young ruler went away and was lost to view. Peter went on with Jesus. Once when talking with a group of children who were joining the church, I said, "If a time came when you knew you had made a bad mistake and you wanted to tell it to somebody and you could go to one of the apostles, which one would you go to?" A young boy flashed back the answer, "To Peter." I said, "Why?" He replied, "Because he made mistakes too, and he would understand." Yes, Peter made mistakes, but he attained qualities of soul and he led people. The person who never makes any mistakes is usually the person who has never dared anything. Never having dared, he has no mistakes registered against him. Such a man does not make mistakes, he is a mistake.

Peter did things. He preached that sermon at Pentecost that swept 3000 people into the Kingdom of God. He made his way to Rome and the best tradition says that he closed his work by being crucified—crucified head downward at his own request, because he did not feel worthy to be crucified head upward as had been his Lord. Nevertheless, he lives. Simon became Peter, the shifting sand became solid rock. His record and his name endure.

Jesus did not give Peter an easy way. But he opened the way to life at its best. You are not asking for the easy way. You are asking for life in its finest form. In Jesus it can be realized. The glorious paradox about life with Jesus is that in slavery to Him we gain liberty, and in seeking to do His will and His work unconsciously there slip into the soul through windows and doors the very best rewards of life.

In Shakespeare's story of King Lear, he pictures the Earl of Kent, coming in disguise to the King.

Says King Lear, "What do you want?"

Replies the Earl of Kent, "I would serve you."

Says King Lear, "Why?"

Then comes that famous answer of the Earl of Kent,

"Because there is that in your countenance that I would fain call master."

Says King Lear, "What is it?"

Answers the Earl of Kent, "Authority."

Peter knew that there was the authority of Divine and Eternal Truth in Jesus. He put himself under that authority. That is what made him Peter, beloved of the Church forever. That will make us too, and lead us to the best that life can know and be and do.

XII

JOHN THE BAPTIST

The Decision To Witness

"And this is the witness of John, when the Jews sent unto him from Jerusalem priests and Levites, to ask him, Who art thou? And he confessed and denied not; and he confessed, I am not the Christ. I am the voice of one crying in the wilderness, Make straight the way of the Lord."—JOHN 1:19-20 and 23.

"Verily I say unto you, Among them that are born of women, there hath not arisen a greater than John the Baptist."—MATTHEW 11:11.

THESE two scripture selections portray two great persons giving their witness concerning each other. John the Baptist is witnessing to the Messiahship of Jesus. Jesus is witnessing to the greatness of John, the prophet of the wilderness.

93

Matthew, in the eleventh chapter, which tells the story of the imprisonment of John the Baptist on the authority of Herod Antipas, reveals John in painful doubt about Jesus. John's message to Jesus said, "Art thou he that should come or look we for another?"

John was enduring the hardships of imprisonment, very likely at Herod's castle of Machærus, east of the Dead Sea. John was constitutionally a man of energy and action and time; inaction and the ministry of Jesus troubled his mind. In the preaching of John he reveals two ideas about the Messiah which he could not see being fulfilled in Jesus. One was that the Messiah would be a swift and complete reformer. The ax was already lying at the root of the tree. The Messiah would take it up and use it to cut down all unworthy trees. Changing the figure of speech, John said, "He will gather the wheat into his garner, but the chaff he will burn with unquenchable fire." That is a picture of a thoroughgoing reformer. That pictures fearless action. But Jesus, instead of working with ax and fire against evil situations, was speaking in the kindly terms of a popular preacher. He was surrounded by admiring crowds. Then John expected of the Messiah that He would be a sufferer. The Messiah's attitudes on questions of belief and behavior must necessarily mean suffering. But, instead of suffering, John heard that Jesus was a guest of honor at a dinner party, a central figure at a lavishly spread table, among publicans and sinners. In Jesus, John could see neither reformer nor sufferer. Thus he sent two messengers to ask, "Art thou he that should come, or look we for another?" The trouble with John was that he was impatient. Every reformer is. John wanted to see changes forcibly brought about overnight. Those changes did not come. Jesus might have given John a clear statement that He was the Messiah. Jesus, however, did the finer and stronger thing. He asked John to think long and searchingly about what he was saying and doing. Therein John would discover the Redeemer who would indeed be also the reformer.

When the messengers of John went away Jesus said, "Among them that are born of women there hath not arisen a greater than John the Baptist." John the Baptist said, in turn, "I am not the Christ" . . . "There cometh one mightier than I" . . . "Behold the Lamb of God."

John Brought to His Work as the Witness to the Messiahship of Jesus the Qualities Which Jesus Calls Great. John was thoroughly sincere. He was genuinely honest. Robert Burns once said, quoting another, "An honest man's the noblest work of God." To understand John it is wise to look at the picture that Luke gives of John's parents. Jesus condemned certain priests at the temple, but there were those who were different. Zacharias and his wife Elisabeth lived in the hill country of Judea. They were far different from the faithless men who controlled the temple. When Zacharias took his turn at the temple, as Luke describes it in the first chapter of his beautiful gospel, the people met with a priest who was different. Here was a man of quality. And here was a priest's wife of quality. Luke says, "They were both righteous before God, walking in all the commandments and ordinances of the Lord blameless," (Luke 1:6). That is a statement about nobility of character. It is one thing to live blameless before our neighbors. But to live in the searching light of God and to be found blameless there— that tells of strong and transparent goodness. In such a home John grew up. That home was in the hill country. "Thy righteousness, O Lord, is as the great mountains." John learned the lessons about life's best qualities up there in that noble and godly highland home. There was the rugged strength of the hills in him. He was God's man.

John brought understanding to his ministry. Very likely he had gone to Jerusalem with his parents. He saw and felt the insincerity and the emptiness of all that was so gorgeous and elaborate in the outside and so corrupt in the inside. He was not deceived. His parents were godly and good. The temple was godless and corrupt. When the day came for John to leave home and take his place in the world, it was not as a priest but as a preacher. It was a long time since a real preacher had been heard in the land. The unknown preacher whose sermons of encouragement and faith are embodied in the book of Daniel had been heard nearly two hundred years before. That preacher had greatly helped the religious and patriotic work of Judas Maccabæus. But since then the preacher's voice was faint or not heard. Now John burst like an Elijah on the scene. He had no church. His church was the open air beside the river of Jordan, and strangely enough near the spot where the children of Israel entered their Promised Land. His food is the simple fare of the wilderness, such things as could be gathered in from trees and bushes, such as locusts and wild honey. The locust may not have been the locust that became a pest. It may have been an edible berry or leaf from the locust tree. John's pulpit probably was a rock. And then the discerning man declared that although the temple priests knew it not, the very Kingdom of God was at hand.

John put an unselfish purpose into his life and work. When you find a man who is unselfishly committed to a great and good purpose, you find a man who is made by that purpose. The man is so overwhelmingly captivated by the purpose that he is quite unconscious of what he himself is becoming. He steadily grows, he constantly expands in the magnitude of a mighty personality. That was what happened to John. No wonder that the people came from villages, towns, and cities, people by the thousands, to hear this wilderness preacher. Ralph Waldo Emerson has been credited with the remark, "If a man make a better mousetrap than his neighbor, the world will make a beaten path to his door." In the case of John the Baptist it was the better sermon. If John was unconscious of his greatness, the people were not. They knew that some person who was as Elijah's spirit was preaching there by the Jordan, and they went in multitudes to hear him.

John put courage into his life and work. It was very likely too that John was quite unconscious of being courageous. He simply gave himself in sincere and whole-hearted fashion to the purposes of God. The outreach of that was that the great controlling purpose swept all fear out of his soul and he never asked "Is it safe to say or do this?" He simply asked "Is it right?"

What Was the Nature of John's Witness? John witnessed to the deadliness of sin. He saw the peoples' sin as their own worst enemies. Sin was like a rotten tree that cumbered the ground and which the blow of an ax must remove. Sin was like the chaff at a threshing. It was useless and a nuisance. It must be burned up. No religion is adequate that stops short of dealing with the question of sin. By the same token, no religion is adequate that does not deal with the whole range of personal and corporate life. It has to do with a man's personal life in his own home, and it has to do with a government's undertakings with the government of another nation.

John witnessed to the Messiahship of Jesus. We reach a point in the ministry of Jesus where we hear Peter say, "Thou art the Christ, the Son of the living God." Rightly that has been called "the Great Confession." It was not, however, the original confession or discovery of the Messiahship of Jesus. John found that out. When Jesus came to John asking for baptism, John recognized as he looked into the face and eyes of the Nazarene that he was dealing with Somebody who was different. John had been baptizing many men. Now he hesitated and said, "I have need to be baptized of thee, and comest thou to me?" Jesus would have it thus. Jesus was baptized. But John could not keep his eyes

97

from Jesus. He saw as it were a dove from heaven. In his very soul he heard the very voice of God saying, "This is my beloved Son, in whom I am well pleased." The Son of God was the Messiah. Then, on a day after the temptation of Jesus after the forty days in the wilderness, John sees Jesus returning to his church of the open air. As Jesus steps in over the rim of the wilderness, fresh from his great victory, his face radiant with the brightness of God, John stops in his preaching. He not only stops—he points his listeners and especially he points his own disciples to Jesus, and says, "Behold the Lamb of God which taketh away the sin of the world." Here is the Messiah in His redemptive enterprise. Surely this is John at his best. He virtually says to his men, "This is the one of whom I have told you. See him. Now you are to leave me and follow him. Behold the Lamb of God." A little later, in another place, further north, Ænon, John was told that men were following Jesus. John said that for men to turn from him to Jesus was as it ought to be. "He must increase but I must decrease," (John 3:30). John was the announcer, going ahead to say, "Prepare ye the way of the Lord."

John's Witness Was to the Necessity of Repentance. Repentance is a complete about turn in life. It is a man going in one direction, and he stops, turns around, and goes in the opposite direction. That message of repentance took in everybody. It took in the people in general, for "he came unto all the region round about Jordan, preaching the baptism of repentance unto remission of sins." The message of repentance was directed to the Pharisees and Sadducees who came to his baptism, and he said, "Ye offspring of vipers, who warned you to flee from the wrath to come? Bring forth therefore fruit worthy of repentance" (Matthew 3: 7-8). Dr. David Smith, in his vivid portrayal of the life of Jesus, says of this message of John to the Pharisees and Sadducees, "As John looked at them, he thought of a scene

98

which he had often witnessed in the wilderness, when the parched brushwood caught fire and the reptiles rushed from their lairs in mad terror. 'Ye offspring of vipers!' he cried, 'who hath warned you to flee from the wrath to come?' " *
The message of repentance was directed to Herod Antipas. Herod Antipas had wronged the whole nation in a political dictatorship and a personal behavior which cruelly hurt the people. John went straight to Herod and rebuked him. Very likely Josephus preserves the explanation which Herod gave for the arrest of John when he says that the crowds who gathered around the fiery reformer were a political menace. That is altogether likely what Herod Antipas intended should be given as the explanation. The real cause for the arrest of John the Baptist was that John had rebuked Herod for taking his brother Philip's wife, Herodias. Herodias was an evil woman who never gave up her plotting against John until she had had him beheaded. It is far better simply to refer to the cruel story than to retell it. But still, from the death cell of John the Baptist came the call to Herod Antipas to repent. The fact that, when he heard about the preaching of Jesus, Herod suspected it to be John back from the dead is evidence that the penetrating message of John had really disturbed his soul. John was not, however, really killed. He was released by that death. All the ages since then and yet to be will hear his message, "Repent, for the kingdom of heaven is at hand."

The message of John was one of confidence in God's enterprise of human redemption. John went back to the preaching of the great Prophet of the Exile for language to express his faith in the enterprise of the grace of God that would claim a wayward people of earth as His own. John saw the thrust of this mighty grace of God in the life of earth's sin-blighted humanity, as he repeated,

* From *The Days of His Flesh,* by David Smith, p. 30. By permission of A. C. Armstrong & Sons, New York.

"Make ye ready the way of the Lord,
Make his paths straight.
Every valley shall be filled
And every mountain and hill shall be brought low;
And the crooked shall become straight,
And the rough ways smooth;
And all flesh shall see the salvation of God"
(Isaiah 40:2-5).

That vivid poetry is the statement of a great faith in God and His enterprise of human redemption. It is like building a highway through a difficult country. Hills of earth and stone are cut through and the earth and stone are thrown into swamps. Then the valleys are exalted and the hills brought low. Moreover, deadly curves are eliminated and the straightened road is made clear for travelers. The rough spots are paved and made smooth. That means work. So does human redemption. It is an enterprise for God and man in union. But it can be done. Perhaps the very war will blast away hilly obstacles from human progress and toss them into seas. Perhaps race prejudice and pride of empire and the narrow isolationism of those who think they can live as a nation to themselves will be eliminated. Perhaps the very war will help prepare a highway for God. It can be that. Then we shall realize the universal love of God, universal brotherhood, and the universal leadership of Jesus so that the vision of John will become reality—"Repent for the kingdom of heaven is at hand."

XIII

THE RICH YOUNG RULER
The Decision To Play Safe

"If thou wouldst enter into life, keep the commandments."
—MATTHEW 19:17.

"But when the young man heard the saying, he went away sorrowful, for he was one that had great possessions."—MATTHEW 19:22.

WHEN Jesus spoke to the rich young ruler concerning keeping the Commandments, the implications went far deeper than a formal or even complete obedience to a list of written statements. The Commandments are those deep, underlying principles of life which, when obeyed, lead to more abundant living, and which, when disobeyed, lead to death. Indeed, if the written Ten Commandments were complete and sufficient, there would have been no need of Jesus and the Beatitudes. The Commandments mark a great achievement in the art of living. The Beatitudes are the life principles that go deeper than the Commandments.

We cannot avoid the eternal laws of life. They are the environment of life. By law one does not mean some regulation concerning behavior under given circumstances. That regulation may prove at length to be unwise and untrue. Indeed, the greatest of men have smashed regulations in order to live in harmony with the laws of God, of the universe, and of human life.

Real liberty comes by understanding the laws of life and working with them. To violate the laws of heat or cold is not to break those laws, but to see them work to our own hurt or destruction. We are frozen or burned. To work with them is to know comfort and security. To violate the law of gravitation is not to break it. Rather the law breaks us, as any foolish attempt to step from a window out over a street results in a broken body on the pavement below. To obey the law of gravitation and to use it wisely is to put power at our disposal for creative work.

Thus Jesus saw the meaning and the outreach of the Commandments, those eternal laws within which and by the help of which we can know life at its best. As they bear on living with God and people, Jesus summarized it all by saying, "Thou shalt love the Lord thy God with all thy heart and mind and soul and strength and thy neighbor as thyself." The laws of God are laws of love and they are God expressing Himself. To obey them—that way lies life.

What are the implications of Jesus' saying, "Keep the commandments"? For the answer we must look for the principles which do lie deeper than the specific regulation.

Surely it means to take life seriously. That does not mean a ban on fun. Play is just as necessary to life as work. But it does mean that we shall see that life is not just a continual picnic. It is a noble and serious business. One of our weaknesses is that we go to an extreme on a good thing, leaving out the opposite good thing, until a good thing has bad results for us. Work is perfectly good for us, but work alone will make life mere drudgery. Play is a good thing, but play alone will make life a mere picnic. Let both work and play do their good offices in making us. We are taking life seriously when we let play have its turn at making life interesting, beautiful, and resilient. We shall work all the better for it. Play adds to life what architecture adds to a building. The cave dwellers were content with mere protection over their heads. They ignored ventilation and beauty. Architecture adds beauty to utility. When we hold work and play in proper perspective we are taking life seriously.

Discipline is one of these underlying laws of life. Discipline is an enlargement of the word disciple. No one would need to argue with the army the necessity of discipline. Without discipline our fighting forces would be mobs of armed men fighting among themselves. They would very soon become savage bandits. Discipline lies at the very base of military or naval efficiency. No discipline, no army; no discipline, no navy. No one would need to argue with a football team the need of discipline. Leave out discipline and there simply is no team, for team work would be impossible.

Discipline from an external power, like the discipline imposed on a regiment is necessary. Discipline that is inner and personal is something finer still. There are branches of the military and naval service where, in the nature of the service, each man must be very largely his own officer. That is often true in a branch like the Signal Corps. Oftentimes in that the individual must be utterly self-directed. The welfare of a division can easily turn on the capacity of the man to act with intelligence, initiative, and dependability. Men who cannot bring to that branch of the service the quality of self-discipline are not very valuable, or, at least, they must be assigned to work where routine duties are all that are expected of them.

The matter of discipline carries over into the matter of life as a son of God. The place where God's laws are written are on the tablets of the hearts of the sons of God. Government is from within. "If thou wouldst enter into life, keep that law of inner discipline."

The right use of time goes into the matter of keeping the Commandments. Time is both a wrecker and a builder. Time pulls down mountains and carries them off into the ocean. The Laurentian Mountains across Quebec, north of the Ottawa River, are considered by geologists to be the oldest mountains in the world. One reason for that conclusion is that no fossils are found there. There is no fossil of a leaf or an animal to tell the story of vegetable and animal life. These mountains are very old. They are now mere stumps of hills compared with the Rockies. Even yet the brown stream of the Ottawa River is carrying the soil of the Laurentian Mountains into the St. Lawrence and off to the sea. From where the Ottawa River enters the St. Lawrence the brown waters of the Ottawa can be distinguished for a long distance in the clearer waters of the St. Lawrence.

Time pulls down mountains. Time is tearing down the Rocky Mountains. They are tumbling down as fast as they can fall and are being carried by countless streams to the ocean. Time also builds. Time is building the earth. An earthquake is the old earth in the process of shaking itself together a little more tightly at a given point. When men build their homes over spots where that work is unfinished, they are often suddenly and disastrously disturbed by an earthquake.

Time builds as well as destroys. It is a builder in life as well as in the earth. It is our possession. What are we doing with it? We have not limitless time on earth. It is very limited. When I heard one man refer to "Life's Long Trail," it was to hear his friend flash back the reply, "You mean 'Life's Short Trail.'" Morning is so quickly noonday. Then noonday is afternoon, and the shadows of evening come so terribly soon. Men and women who have made worthy persons of themselves and have done worthy things have known how to use wisely their time.

Such a person was Booker T. Washington. The young Negro lad did not know who his father was, and his mother was a slave. When he started to school and his name was asked for, he didn't have any name to give, and he replied, "Booker Washington." That name remained with him for life. As a boy he went to work in a mine and in his spare time he attended a night school. He heard two miners talking about a certain great school somewhere for colored boys. It was in Virginia. He decided to go. At Richmond he slept under a wooden sidewalk with his little satchel as a pillow.

When at last he reached Hampton and the school he had fifty cents in his pocket with which to begin his education. He waited his turn to be interviewed as an applicant for admission. After some hours, the teacher interviewing him said, "The adjoining room needs sweeping." That young Negro set to work. He swept the room three times and dusted it four times. He said later that he believed then that his whole future turned on how he cleaned that room. He moved back furniture and cleaned behind the furniture, cleaned every out-of-the-way spot. He not only cleaned the room, he polished it. Then the teacher came to examine it. Although she rubbed her handkerchief over woodwork and furniture, and peered into corners, she found no dust anywhere. The lad was admitted and given work as a janitor. He worked part of the time at cleaning and the rest of the time—his spare time—he studied. The result of that use of time was inevitable. He became a God-given leader of his people—Booker T. Washington.

If a young Negro lad, with so little to give him incentive, with so little background—not even a name—could make of himself Booker T. Washington and do what he did, what is open to the boys and girls who have our great high schools of today and time at their disposal?

> "Time worketh, let me work, too,
> Time undoeth, let me do;
> Busy as time, my work I ply,
> Till I rest in the rest of Eternity."

It was a wise man of the Psalms who knew this underlying law about the use of time, who prayed, "So teach me to number my days [value my time] that I may apply my heart unto wisdom."

A well-defined purpose is surely one of those laws of life— an underlying "command." Purpose and vocation are twins. It is not good enough for our young people simply to drift into life's work. They must have the opportunity to study and appraise their own powers and to match those against the needs of the world. Out of that will come purpose and vocation. The objective can easily be made, now that the global war is smashing the plans of our young people. Yet within that we are not losing sight of the deeper law, and those who are determined to be and to do will not allow even the war to stop their progress. It is a wise government that provides education in the armed forces for that day beyond the war as well as training for victory. Victory alone is not enough. If we would enter into the fuller life of peace we must "keep the commandments," that is, we must see and help our soldiers and sailors to see a purpose and a vocation in the years beyond.

Then surely there is this mighty thing: the person who will enter into life must never turn his back on truth. To see larger truth, and because of laziness, fear, or refusal to be disturbed—to be deliberately blind to it and disobey it—that way lies tragedy, the tragedy of slavery. Said Jesus, "The truth shall make you free."

What about an adequate test for life? For Himself, Jesus said, "I am come that you might have life and have it more abundantly." Surely He was saying that the life and effort which enriched life for all was the real life—that a person who follows truth has entered into life. It is not going to be an easy way. It will, indeed, often be a way of suffering and perhaps suffering at the hands of friends who do not want to see you suffer. To such must come the answer of Jesus which He gave to friends who warned him about what Herod Antipas would do to Him:

"Go and say to that fox, Behold, I cast out devils and perform cures today and tomorrow, and the third day I am perfected. Howbeit, I must go on my way today and to-morrow and the day following: for it cannot be that a prophet perish out of Jerusalem" (Luke 13:32-33).

The Decision to Play Safe Was the Reply of the Rich Young Ruler to the Call of Jesus to Enter into Life. All that the record says is, "He went away sorrowful, for he had great possessions." Where did the young man go? Back to his wealth and ease, back to his place of local prestige and authority, back to an aching conscience and unsatisfied soul, back to the living death of playing safe.

The choice is ours. Nobody can make the decision for us. When we meet Jesus we come to a cross-roads of life, where we must make a decision that carves out destiny.

The rich Young Ruler decided to play safe. When Hofmann painted the picture he put the tragedy of the "play safe" decision in the features of the young man. He put the pain of knowing the meaning of that decision in the face of Jesus.

It can all be so different if we will have a best way and dare to go with Him, at whatever cost, as we hear Him say, "He that will lose his life shall save it"; "If thou wouldest enter into life, keep the commandments"—live by God's laws of life, which laws are alive and sovereign and rewarding in all that Jesus is. "I am come that they might have life and that they might have it more abundantly." . . . "Sell that thou hast and give to the poor, and come, follow me."

XIV

ANDREW
The Decision To Live Helpfully

"One of the two that heard John speak, and followed Jesus, was Andrew, Simon Peter's brother."—JOHN 1:40.

THE few pictures we have of Andrew in the gospels are given to us by John. In the other three gospels he appears only as a name among other names. The places where John enables us to see Andrew in action are so beautifully interesting that we long for more to complete the picture. What we do see of Andrew tells us of a man who found his best satisfaction in living helpfully.

The Scottish people have made St. Andrew their patron saint. The St. Andrew's Cross of Scotland was blended with the St. George's Cross of England to make the first Union Jack. It was that "Jack" of the two crosses which was seen in America in the days of the Revolutionary War. The entrance of the third cross, the Irish Cross of St. Patrick, came at the end of the eighteenth century.

Scotland has cherished her legends of St. Andrew. Tradition has it that Andrew was crucified at Patras, Achæa on a saltire-shaped cross, now the St. Andrew's Cross. That tradition relates that the relics of St. Andrew were first taken to Constantinople. Later, A.D. 731, they were removed to Scotland, to Muckross, the city of the King of the Picts, Angus Macfergus. Very quickly St. Andrew became the patron saint of the Scottish people. Then the name of the city, Muckross, gave way to the new name, St. Andrews. A later story, related by Sir Harris Nichols in his *History of the Order of the Thistle,* tells that A.D. 987 Achaius, King of the Scots, was marching at the head of 10,000 soldiers in an expedition to assist Hungus, King of the Picts, against

Athelstane, King of the West Saxons. The Scottish king and his chieftains spent a night in prayer. Against the background of the blue sky they saw white clouds take the form of the Cross of St. Andrew. Their prayers were heard and would be answered. They went forward with confidence. St. Andrew's Cross became the "jack" or "flag" of Scotland.

Thus the sainted Apostle Andrew lives in the legends of the Scottish people. No wonder that many of the churches of the Scottish people have claimed his name to adorn their meeting places. In the city of Toronto the Scottish residents built an "Old St. Andrews" and a "New St. Andrews."

Andrew Was a Seeker. When Roger Williams left the fellowship of the Baptists in Providence, Rhode Island, he called himself a "seeker."

A patient, sincere seeker comes into actual possession of much that the rest of us miss. One of the best relaxations I have discovered is to go into the woods with a friend who has been "seeking" among the trees and beside the streams for years. He is still seeking. One spring day I had broken off work for a few hours and had gone with him into the woods. We had just well entered among the trees when he said, "Hello, here it is, the hepatica. I wonder if the buds have come." He laid back the dead leaves of the winter from the green leaves of the little flower which was struggling up among them, and said, "Yes, here it is. The bud is just ready to break; the hepatica is the first of them all." My friend went on to quote John Burroughs, the great naturalist:

"There are many things left for May, but nothing fairer than, if as fair as, the first flower, the hepatica. I find I have never admired this little firstling half enough. When at the maturity of its charm, it is certainly the gem of the woods." *

* From *New Nature Library,* Vol. 8, p. 18.

Then this lover of the woods lapsed into poetry, quoting the lines,

> "Blue as the heaven it gazes at,
> Startling the loiterer in the naked groves
> With unexpected beauty; for the time
> Of blossoms and green leaf is not yet." *

Next we stopped at a fern, and my friend looked at the design on the underside of the leaf, and said, "This fern, the leatherwood, has kept wonderfully green under the snow." On we wandered, and then he said, "Listen." I listened carefully, and then at last I heard what his keen ear had already heard, the distant tones of frogs—the deep guttural tones of the wood frog, and the sharp, shrill tones of the hyla frog. This lover of the out-of-doors, this seeker in the woods, said, "The wood frog croaks, not from disgust or disdain, as humans often do; he croaks to express his love." Soon we actually saw the frogs in pond and stream. They had been up out of the winter mud only for the last few hours. The seeker did not miss them. Then my woodland guide pointed out to me, at the bottom of a little stream, a moving twig. It was no larger than a small pencil, and about two inches long. But it was moving upstream. He put his hand into the water and lifted it out. He said, "This is a caddish fly; it takes its own house along with it at the bottom of the stream. Soon it will leave that house and you will see it on the surface of the water." We walked on. He said, "Look—the first bluebird; not the bluejay, but the bluebird—the first of the spring." As we wandered on, my friend would bend over the branch of a bush and talk to a bud just ready to burst into life. He stopped at a moss bank and knelt, with his glass in his hand, his eyes and spirit thrilled by the delicate beauty of a patch of moss. That man is a seeker and that woods, where most of us would walk without seeing much beyond

* From *New Nature Library,* Vol. 8, p. 17.

the bare trees and dead leaves and patches of water, is to him a universe where life and beauty are speaking in the wonder and design of God's own beneficent care.

Andrew was a "seeker" in the days of John the Baptist and Jesus. He sought out John the Baptist. He listened to what John had to say about the Kingdom of God and the coming Messiah. Then one day, while John was preaching, Jesus came back over the rim of the wilderness, fresh from His victory over temptation, and John stopped preaching. He looked toward Jesus. Then Andrew heard John say, "Behold the Lamb of God." John was really telling Andrew to leave him and follow after Jesus. Noble John! "He must increase, but I must decrease."

Andrew, the "seeker," followed Jesus. Jesus said, "What seek ye?" Andrew replied, "Master, where dwellest thou?" Jesus said, "Come and see." That was an invitation to follow on. That seeker followed on, and before the few hours' visit with Jesus were over, Andrew had become Jesus' man forever.

Andrew Was a Learner. That is one of the meanings of discipleship. A man who is a disciple of another is a learner from him. What a teacher Andrew had! And what a student Jesus had! When Jesus and Andrew met, that was a University of Christian Life. All that is meant by the Beatitudes—that was what Andrew was learning. It was life according to the idea of God.

One of the very difficult lessons for Andrew to learn, surely, was the lesson of humility. Andrew was in a very difficult position. There is a story in the twenty-third chapter of the second book of Samuel which tells of a man in a position very similar to that of Andrew. David had three mighty men—the first three—who were near him. Their names were Adino, Eleazar, and Shammah. They were mighty men in battle. David wanted water from the well by the gate of Bethlehem. These three mighty men were the

111

ones who stole through the lines of the Philistines, putting their very lives in jeopardy, and brought the water back to David. Then there was Benaiah. Watch Benaiah for the Old Testament counterpart of Andrew. He too was mighty in battle. He fought with men and he fought with beasts. Next to the three mighty men there were thirty choice and valiant men. It was said of Benaiah, "He was more honorable than the thirty, but he attained not to the first three. And David set him over his guard." Benaiah and Andrew are spiritual kinsmen. Not of the first three was Andrew, but easily at the head of the next group of nine. That was Andrew's position. His brother, Simon Peter, and the two brothers, James and John, were of the inner circle—the first three. Andrew was not included in that inner council. He was not included in the group who were taken into Jesus' place of prayer in the Garden of Gethsemane. What an opportunity for the envious heart to complain, for the jealous spirit to rebel. But Andrew accepted his position,

> "Content to follow his Master's plan,
> Love unstinted to every man;
> Content if at most the world would say,
> He helped his brothers along the way."

Love envieth not. This man so thoroughly loved Jesus that to help constantly was his chief joy. He sought neither rank nor position, but a place where he could lift a burden from another's back, or wipe a tear from another's eye. That was Andrew.

Andrew Was a Faithful Man. Once I heard the remark concerning Andrew, "He was like the postage stamp on your letter. He stuck to his job right through to the end." Right through to the end! See the picture of the seven who meet Jesus on the shore of the Lake of Galilee, when the cross and empty tomb are left behind, and Andrew is there. Andrew is there, waiting for further orders from his Master.

The faithful man is the man who is full of faith. Such

112

was Andrew. In his spirit he had made a life adventure with Jesus, and there was no turning back. The last great requirement of God of His servants is not success, as a newspaper counts success, but what God calls "faithfulness." "It is required in stewards that a man be found faithful."

In my hearing, two men were discussing men for a certain position of trust. Concerning one man it was said, "He is brilliant, but he is flighty and he is very apt to let you down at the critical point." Concerning the other it was said, "There is nothing very flashy about him, but he is dependable. You can count on him standing by the job." "The other" was given the appointment, for in the hard spots of an enterprise, dependability is far more valuable than mere brilliance. We pray with Ellen E. Burman,

"Teach me that harder lesson, how to live;
    To serve Thee in the darkest paths of life;
Arm me for conflict now, fresh vigor give,
    And make me more than conqueror in the strife.

"Teach me to live, Thy purpose to fulfill;
    Bright for Thy glory let my taper shine;
Each day renew, remould my stubborn will;
    Closer round Thee my heart's affections twine.

"Teach me to live, no idler let me be,
    But in Thy service hand and heart employ,
Prepared to do Thy bidding cheerfully:
    Be this my highest and my holiest joy.

"Teach me to live, my daily cross to bear,
    Nor murmur though I bend beneath its load;
Only be with me; let me feel Thee near;
    Thy smile sheds gladness on the darkened road.

"Teach me to live, with kindly words for all,
    Wearing no cold, repulsive brow of gloom;
Waiting with cheerful patience till Thy call
    Summon my spirit to its heavenly home."

That was Andrew—faithful.

Andrew Was a Winner. He was a winner in his own personal life. He was also a winner for the Kingdom. See Andrew in three great avenues of Christian enterprise.

Andrew promoted Christian friendliness. It was in the northern wilderness, and five thousand people had been listening to Jesus. Food ran short. Who was it that made the suggestion that was the key to the solution of the difficulty? None other than Andrew. "There is a lad here with five barley loaves and a few small fishes." The lad was ready to share. The result was that everyone else who had supplies shared with those who were without food, and all were cared for. Christian friendliness works that miracle on the minds of people, where the miracle is needed, and satisfaction follows. In this day of cruelty and hardness it is the Christian friendliness of Andrew that must lead the way to better things in the days beyond the war. Oh for Andrews! A London preacher once remarked, "I am quite willing for Thomas to go to City Temple and Simon Zelotes to Whitefield's, but let me have a church of Andrews." Andrew's life was one of Christian friendliness. "Do you know," said E. O. Excell—

"Do you know the world is dying
      For a little bit of love?
Everywhere we hear them sighing
      For a little bit of love:
For the love that rights a wrong,
Fills the world with joy and song.
They have waited, oh, so long
      For a little bit of love."

More than that, Andrew was a personal evangelist on the home front. No sooner had he made the great discovery concerning Jesus than he went to his brother to say, "We have found the Messiah." We never read of Andrew preaching a sermon. There is not a sermon in the New Testament credited to Andrew. But when Andrew brought his brother

114

Simon to Jesus, he brought the preacher of Pentecost, whose sermons in the streets of Jerusalem swept people into the Kingdom by the thousands. The Church can never pay its debt of gratitude to the Andrew-minded people of her fellowship. They are never heard in platform speeches. They seldom make or second a resolution that is written into the records of the secretary of the convention. But they are resolutions incarnate. They are resolutions that live. They have patiently taught in the church school. They have talked it all out with doubters and with those who have troubled hearts and with those who are broken by sin. They have gone to people's homes and listened and prayed. Above all, they have lived it out. The result has been that Peters have been released into the life and work of the church, Peters who went up into the company of "the first three." They had been introduced to Jesus by the Andrews of our fellowship. The Andrews are the real "pillars" of the Church.

Beyond that, Andrew had an interest further afield than the Jewish race. When certain Greeks came to Jerusalem and said to Philip, "Sir, we would see Jesus," it was Andrew who made very sure that the Greeks did meet Jesus. Jesus saw in those Greeks the early comers from the Gentile world, who would eventually make up such an area of His Kingdom.

Yes, Andrew touched all the three great regions of the work of the modern church in her outreach to humanity. He was a missionary of Christian friendliness. He was a missionary of home and personal evangelism. He was a missionary with an eye for those of other races and of other tongues and colors. In all these great lines of endeavor of the Christian Church it is the Andrews who are our choice, dependable and effective men.

Andrew decided that matter of Christian helpfulness when he decided to "follow Jesus." In the National Art Gallery of London, on a day after the close of the First World War, an American officer was standing looking at a painting of the Christ carrying His cross to Golgotha. Then he knew by his feelings that there was a person standing near him. Turning round, his eyes met a young American soldier, who had been badly wounded in battle. The soldier was lame, and walked with the help of a cane, and the wound stripes on his arm told the story of his fighting at the front. The young soldier stood at attention, gave his salute to the Christ of Calvary, and then remarked in deep, determined tones, "Jesus of Nazareth, in the work Thou hast to do in this world, count on me."

Such a decision it is our high privilege in our day to make, with its outreach of destiny for ourselves and others. What Andrew did and what he became and the helpfulness of his work—all that calls to us, in the words of Cecil F. Alexander,

> "As of old, St. Andrew heard it
>   By the Galilean lake,
>   Turned from home and toil and kindred,
>   Leaving all for His dear sake."

XV

NICODEMUS

The Decision To Know

"Nicodemus answered and said unto him, How can these things be?"—JOHN 3:9.

NICODEMUS was a member of the Sanhedrin, as was his companion, Joseph of Arimathea. Any power which the Roman imperial power had left in the hands of the Jews had been vested in the Sanhedrin. The power of those seventy men, however, stopped short of the authority to render a death sentence, which accounts for the necessity of taking Jesus to Pilate.

The fact that Nicodemus, the Sanhedrist, sought out an opportunity to interview Jesus meant that official Jerusalem was uncomfortably conscious of the preaching of Jesus. It was a night interview, perhaps outside the city of Jerusalem.

The story of Jesus and Nicodemus is a three-panel picture. It is the gospel of John alone which gives the pictures.

The First Panel Is The Picture Of An Anxious Pharisee Seeking To Know More About Jesus And His Message. The days of our Lord's ministry were so filled because of the demands of people upon Him, and because of His preaching, that a night interview became necessary if Nicodemus could have any time adequate for his purpose. It may be that Nicodemus was glad of the night hour because of a degree of timidity, for he would be the object of some critical concern on the part of those who were already unfriendly to Jesus.

One wonders to what extent, however, Nicodemus may have been an emissary. As there had been a very evident attempt on the part of official Jerusalem to get control of John the Baptist, was there a similar attempt to control Jesus? Perhaps so. Nicodemus may have been a go-between attempting to negotiate an understanding between this great Galilean preacher, influencing the people, and the Sanhedrin.

Beyond any official action, Nicodemus was concerned for himself. He was a man who had seen that Jesus was a person sent from God and that He had things of great importance to say and do. Nicodemus came on his own account. He wanted to know. It is easily possible that the conversation went on all night and that "cometh to the light" refers to the actual sunrise which ended the conference and sent both Jesus and Nicodemus to another day of life and work in Jerusalem.

What Nicodemus learned that night never was forgotten.

I heard and saw a man struggling through a decision because of important new truth which had come to him. He was confronted right there with a decision that meant an eventual destiny of character and usefulness. To ignore what he had learned meant smug comfort; but it also meant deterioration of moral character. To obey what he had learned meant adventure, risk and discomfort; but it also meant the building of a stronger and better man. Beyond that, it meant the contribution which that stronger man could make to other people in the world of his day and succeeding days.

To such a place Nicodemus came that night. The anxious seeker had an experience in which he discovered new truth, saw what he might become and what he might do. He went back to the life of a Pharisee and to his place in the Sanhedrin with conflict raging in his soul. He was a man torn between an old association and a new loyalty.

The Second Panel of the Picture Shows Jesus Teaching the Truth About Regeneration. Our Lord calls it "The New Birth." Said Jesus to Nicodemus, "Marvel not that I say unto thee, Ye must be born again."

The work of human sin makes the new birth a necessity. By whatever name sin is known, it is the same stubborn and destructive fact. In its essence it is a violation of God, ourselves and other people. In its work it is destructive. In the individual life it results in a human wreck. In the world at large it is the destructiveness of global war. Whether in the individual or in the world-wide scene, the central problem of life is sin. The Psalmist was getting at the necessity when he prayed, "Create in me a clean heart, O Lord, and renew a right spirit within me." Great and comprehensive social and economic planning is necessary, but any planning for human decency that will really work must have behind and within it the remade individuals who have renounced sin and given God His place of worship and guidance in

118

their own minds. The new birth is necessary. "Marvel not that I say unto thee, Ye must be born again."

Then Jesus taught the new birth as a possibility because of the work of the grace of God. On the part of man it must mean genuine repentance, a turning away from sin, a change in the direction that the man is going. On the part of God it is the work of grace. "By grace ye are saved through faith; and that not of yourselves; it is the gift of God." Nature displays plenty of pictures of regeneration in the spring. Is it the dragon fly? The larva that is at home under the water rises and, in response to the light and heat of the sun it one day takes wings and plays among the tree tops. The redbud maple has been stark and dormant during the long winter. Then the sun begins to work. There is a stirring within the ground. The sap runs in the trunk, limbs and twigs, and the red buds emerge and soon the tree is alive with leafy green. That analogy from nature helps to picture what happens to man. Man has been made in the image of God. By sin, or through indifference, he has gone into a winter of deadness. Then there are stirrings within the mind. The grace of God—the Eternal Sun—draws at the inner spirit of the man and in the interplay of the spirit of God and the spirit of man a new man is brought to life. "If any man be in Christ, he is a new creation: old things are passed away; behold all things are become new."

Such a remade man is the human unit of the Kingdom of God. Indeed, there is no Kingdom of God on earth without such personal units. There can be no army of the United States without the individual soldiers. And there can be no Kingdom of God without individual men, who are Christ's men, associating themselves as societies and churches to press forward the redemptive enterprises of God. Jesus was inviting Nicodemus to just such an enterprise when He said, "He that doeth truth cometh to the light, that his deeds may be made manifest, that they are wrought in God."

Surely the sun was rising in the east when Jesus said that. It was Jesus saying, "Nicodemus, a new day has dawned in your soul. Walk in the light as a man following the light of God."

The Third Panel of The Picture Shows a Disciple Making His Discipleship Known. Indeed, within this panel there are steps of progress.

The first step is when Jesus made known to Nicodemus the meaning of the new birth and discipleship.

The second step is pictured in the seventh chapter of John (43-53) when Nicodemus protested against the Sanhedrin carrying out an act of physical violence against Jews. He said, "Doth our law judge any man before it hear him?" They intended to drive Nicodemus back into the silence of inaction as they said, "Art thou also of Galilee?"

The third step is pictured in the nineteenth chapter of John (38-42) when Joseph of Arimathea and Nicodemus, both Sanhedrists, give Jesus reverent burial. Both are men of wealth. Joseph provides the new tomb. Nicodemus provides the myrrh and aloes, about a hundred pounds in weight. Ordinarily a pound of spices would be used. Nicodemus provided about a hundred pounds. Was Nicodemus going to an extreme to declare his regret concerning his secret discipleship and thus making his discipleship a declared and open allegiance? Perhaps so.

There is a fourth step pictured outside the Bible. It comes from the apocryphal gospel of Nicodemus. So much that is contained in the apocryphal gospels was discredited that those gospels were not given a place in the New Testament. The gospel of Nicodemus may be right in relating that Nicodemus went to Peter and John and sought baptism. That would make the discipleship of Nicodemus open and avowed. St. Paul declares that such avowal of discipleship is like a dead man coming to life. "Know ye not that so many of us as were baptized into Jesus Christ were baptized into his death? Therefore we are buried with him by baptism into death: that like as Christ was raised up from the dead by the glory of the Father, even so we also should walk in newness of life" (Romans 6:3-4).

The appeal of Jesus is that our discipleship be open and avowed. There are few men but who will allow the grandeur of the life, character, and work of Jesus. In this day, when again the powers of darkness are challenging the powers of light, it is our high responsibility, knowing the truth, to come to and walk by the divine Light. That way lie life and liberty and the Kingdom of God.

> "Here, Lord, I give myself away;
> 'Tis all that I can do."

XVI

THOMAS

The Decision To Believe

"Let us also go, that we may die with him."—JOHN 11:16.
"I will not believe."—JOHN 20:25.
"My Lord and my God."—JOHN 20:28.

WILL you hear three statements that really are the biography of a doubter? All three are from the lips of Thomas, as recorded in the Gospel according to St. John. In untested enthusiasm he said to his companions, "Let us also go that we may die with him." Then when the testing time came, he said, "I will not believe." At last he emerged into certainty and said, "My Lord and my God."

These three statements record the spiritual pilgrimage of a man who went through doubt to faith. Indeed, he went from faith through doubt into new and deeper faith. That, clearly, is the history of all vigorous faith. We begin by accepting without much question what is presented to us, and what we think we see. It is a steady, reliable world in which we are, and it is a steady, reliable society of which we are a part. Then comes a period of stress and strain, and questioning. Questions are hurled at us, and we ask questions of our own. We question everything, from God to the ground. Out of that period we emerge into faith again, faith that is purified, stronger, adventurous. Our first faith was second-hand faith. Our second faith is first-hand faith. We have gone from faith through doubt to faith. That is the experience of men in the Bible. It is the experience of Abraham in the Old Testament and Thomas in the New.

The Experience of Doubt is Inevitable to the Man Who is Alert to the Facts of Life. Do not think that the young student in your home, or the young business man, or the man of affairs who is a member of the church and dares to confide in you his experience of doubt, is a person to be suspected and disciplined. He is a person to be reckoned with, who, because of his quality, is on the way to a purified and larger faith.

What are the Things that Produce Doubt? Sometimes it is shock from human behavior. I might easily go to other quarters for my picture, but I go to my own calling. Ministers of religion are human, like the rest of you, and individuals among them at times are tragic moral failures. The thing that doubles and trebles that tragedy is that people have looked to their minister for spiritual and moral leadership. Now they are shocked, and some of them question the reality of religion at all, as they and their church are held up to public gaze in the newspapers. The marvel of it is that the church rallies from that experience, trusts another man, and goes on. Now, I say I have gone to my own calling for my picture, through courtesy. I might have gone to other callings and beheld the shock that a doctor, or a lawyer, or a teacher has given to those who trusted him. But the fact is, that the inconsistent and cruel and immoral behavior of other people sometimes is the source of doubt.

The experience of doubt may come from new facts that lift themselves on the horizon of the mind. It may be facts about the physical universe wherein we make our home. That was true of the facts related by Copernicus. The sun did not move from east to west, and the world was not flat. Rather men were living on a spinning globe that was not only spinning, but made trips around the sun to produce the seasons. The Church found it very difficult to receive the new facts and retain faith, for the Bible seemed to teach differently. But the facts were accepted and faith was not destroyed, but enlarged. What is true of the behavior of the universe is true of the size of the universe, and the very immensity of it all makes men ask about the nature of and the immensity of a God in whom the whole thing can find an explanation.

New facts about one's own life and personality may be the starting place of doubt. Our young folks come home from college for the vacation. Do not meet that young lad, alert to and engaged by the new facts that have arisen on the horizon of his mind, with a scolding lecture. Listen to him, and be interested. He, too, is on the way to a larger faith.

There are men who are thrown into doubt by hard circumstances. I am thinking only partly of the stiff times some are having due to the present war. It is true that we are looking facts in the face now with a sincerity that perhaps we lacked in the days of peace. But I am thinking of those disharmonies of human experience that come at all times. I met it one day in this form. A father lost his young boy, the pride of his soul, killed by a truck, while just around the corner a wretched, law-breaking racketeer drove off in a big new car. The question he hurled at me was, "If there is a God of justice, why was my little boy taken and a man like that left to curse the community with his lawless behavior?" You have heard that same question, and to meet that man with any hocus-pocus answer is a spiritual crime. As an honest man, I can only tell that father that I have not the complete answer. I can tell him, however, that there is so much that is good and just that I shall trust still where I cannot explain. To lecture a man like that on the sin of doubting is a moral and religious offense. That man is not sinning, he is suffering. He is suffering in love. What he needs is the love of your heart, not the lecture of your head.

Doubt may be traced to a neglect of human and spiritual fellowships. In his perplexity, the man has retired alone and broods over things until the whole situation grows darker. That is exactly what Thomas did. The two on the Emmaus road at least had each other's fellowship, but Thomas went off alone and brooded over his trouble, and he did not stop at doubt. He went further than that. It was flat unbelief. He said, "I will not believe." Yet I do not read of the disciples scolding Thomas. What they did was to get him back into human and spiritual fellowship, for they believed in him.

Right There, When Doubt Is Raging in the Soul, a Man Is Going to Go Down to Tragedy, or Up to Triumph. If he refuses to exercise moral, spiritual, and mental effort, his doubt will deepen, and probably he will run for refuge to moral cynicism. But there is another way that leads on to certainty and to satisfaction.

How, Then, Shall We Find Our Way from Doubt to Faith? I believe the way can be found. Here are some of the marks of the way.

First of all, have patience. Have patience instead of making caustic demands for immediate evidence. The older people get, the more convinced they are that they have not compassed all the evidence. When the great commoner,

124

Gladstone, could not make good his case to an unfriendly Parliament, he said, "I appeal to time." We sometimes speak of broad-mindedness. Patience is not so much broad-mindedness as it is long-mindedness. "In your patience ye shall win your souls."

Then you will do this—you will be courageous enough to look all facts squarely in the face. I say all the facts. You are not asked to leave out of your thinking any of the well-attested facts of the physical sciences or psychology. Indeed, those facts now are on the side of faith in God. The advocate of mechanistic materialism had better not make his appeal today to science, either to the physical sciences or to psychology to make good his claim. Great scientists are affirming faith in the spiritual meaning of the universe. The completest evidence of science today is on the side of belief in God.

What is true of the physical sciences is true also of the mental science of psychology. Psychology is moving on to the idea of personality that Jesus held, and sees man now, not as the slave of forces he cannot control, but as the possible master of them, whose responsibility it is to rise and determine how he shall act, and to determine the character result that will be attained. Psychology is the greatest possible ally of religion in the matter of releasing man from wrong, and harmonizing his life with himself and other people and with God.

Go the whole distance and take in the facts of science. Take in the fact of Jesus. The plain truth is that Jesus changed the course of history because of what He has made men to be and led them to do. Take Jesus out of the history of the past nineteen hundred years, and you must write over again that history and on a lower plane. The world is bad enough yet, but take out of it the spiritual power and purpose of Jesus in human affairs, and the outlook would be black indeed. The international mind and international fellowship that gather around Jesus constitute the hope for a better world after the war. Have patience and take in all the facts.

I see one other mark on the road that leads to faith. It is utter moral honesty, by which a man will undertake moral adventures with what he knows is morally right. That has never been better stated than by Frederick W. Robertson of Brighton. Stopford A. Brooke tells that human story. Robertson himself, in one of his addresses to the working-men of Brighton, portrays what was surely his own experience. He says:

"When everything seems wrapped in hideous uncertainty, I know but one way in which a man may come forth from his agony scatheless. It is by holding fast those things which are certain still—the grand, simple landmarks of morality. In the darkest hour through which a human soul can pass, whatever else is doubtful, this at least is certain: If there be no God and no future state, yet even then, it is better to be generous than selfish, better to be chaste than licentious, better to be true than to be false, better to be brave than to be a coward. His night shall pass into the clear bright day."

That was Robertson's way on to the larger faith. Living in doubt is like going through a fog. It is then that the airplane pilot steers by dead reckoning. That is what I mean. Steer by the dead reckoning of what an honest conscience tells you is the right. Jesus said, "Blessed are the pure in heart, for they shall see"—they shall see the sunlight again, and they shall know God. Purity of heart does not mean moral perfection, else we are all done for. But what it does mean is moral and spiritual sincerity. Adventure with that, and ahead are the sunlight and God.

Grant Me These Two Things: That the noblest way of life you know anything about is what you behold in Jesus and that if you can find God, you will want Him to be like that. Grant me these two things as true for your thinking, and then, with the deepest sincerity, say to that Jesus, "What wilt thou have me to do?" And in that adventure with Him, you will see the sun begin to break through the fog, the skies clear, faith emerge, and you will have gone through doubt to faith, and you too will say, "My Lord and my God," for He is the satisfying answer to all the wild questions of the soul.

XVII

BARNABAS

The Decision To Be a Friend

"But Barnabas took him, and brought him to the apostles, and declared unto them how he had seen the Lord in the way, and that he had spoken to him, and how at Damascus he had preached boldly in the name of Jesus. And he was with them going in and going out at Jerusalem."—Acts 9:27-28.

ONCE I heard an old Scotch preacher preparing his congregation for the Christmas season. Concerning Christmas gifts, he said, "Let your giving be sincere. That gift is a bit of yourself you are giving to other people. Do not make a gift if the symbol is insincere. When you send a gift you are saying, 'It is myself I am offering to you in Christian friendliness.'" I think that if Barnabas were preaching a Christmas sermon in one of our churches he would say something very similar. He saw the Christian life as a sharing life.

It is a gross misunderstanding of the sharing spirit of Barnabas to suppose that he was advocating a particular economic pattern of communism. Such an idea was not in his mind. He was just a man who shared with others all that he was and all that he had.

When, as recorded in Acts 4:36-37, Barnabas sold his

farm and put the money he received into the projects of the church at Jerusalem, it was just his way of sharing things. He was giving everything. That sort of thing won for him his nickname, "Bar-Nabas," meaning "Son of Consolation," or "Son of Encouragement." He must have been a consolation and an encouragement to many.

When Barnabas, as recorded in Acts 9:26-28, brought Saul into the fellowship of the church at Jerusalem, it again was sharing. Already Barnabas had given himself to Saul in Christian friendship, and now he would have Saul share the fellowship of the church. The people of that church were afraid of Saul. They had reason for their fears. They could not believe that Saul was now a disciple. It was Barnabas who went surety for Saul and opened the door of the church to him and made him one of the group.

A few references in the Acts of the Apostles enable us to create a portrait of Barnabas. Apparently he was a tiller of the soil. He owned a farm. He was a man who loved the out-of-doors. At the city of Lystra, Barnabas was called "Jupiter" by the superstitious people, while Paul was called "Mercury." That clearly tells one thing, that physically Barnabas was the larger and more impressive man. Barnabas was a Levite. He belonged to the hereditary priestly class. He became a disciple of Jesus. That released in still finer form all his faculties for useful living. When he was sent as a messenger to the church at Antioch he was described as "a good man, full of the Holy Ghost and of faith."

This man is a fine example of Christian faith and love in the determination to share all good things with others. Behind the enterprise of sharing there are a few strong Christian virtues.

Barnabas Was Genuine. We find no false notes in his life. He was very careful about the sort of person he offered to other people. Real friends always are. They never palm off a fraud on others. When gifts were being made at the

Jerusalem Church, Ananias and Sapphira came, offering their gift. They said that they had given all. That was untrue. Behind the untruth was that treacherous thing, the desire to be given credit for being what we are not and giving what we have not really given. The real offense of these people was that they were offering to the fellowship of the church two lives that were not genuine. The first concern of Barnabas was that he be genuine. When he became a Christian the new lordship in his life went into all parts of his life. There were no reserved rooms where Jesus could not enter. He was not following Jesus with a fraction of his being. He was wholly and genuinely Jesus' man.

Barnabas Had Faith In Other People. That is an essential in Christian usefulness. We can be of little redemptive help to people unless we believe in them. It is not a thing to be surprised at that the people of the Jerusalem church were suspicious of Saul. As Saul of Tarsus he had made havoc of the church. He had stood by when the saintly Stephen was stoned to death—lynched! Then Saul went on his murderous way to Damascus. The people of the church heard that Saul of Tarsus had a change of heart, but they were suspicious and they were cautious. So would this or any other church be if a man who had been an arch enemy suddenly came asking for admission into membership.

But it was the generous-hearted Barnabas who would share the fellowship of the church with Saul. It would be interesting to know how these two men spent their time in Jerusalem. Perhaps they shared the same room in a humble home. Perhaps together they made visits to Gethsemane and Calvary and the Mount of Olives. Then one day Barnabas rose in the fellowship of the church and proposed Saul for membership. How interesting it would be to have the record of what Barnabas said in that motion of recommendation. It was on the assurance of Barnabas that Saul was accepted. We owe to the faith that Barnabas had in another man the fact that Paul entered the church.

Barnabas was able to see the spirit of Jesus working in unusual enterprises. Once we have set up an organization it is very easy for us to suppose that organization must be the permanent standard. What is different from our type is inferior, if, indeed, it is not false. Away up at Antioch a Christian community had sprung into action and was doing very unusual things in different ways. The outspoken feelings of the Jerusalem group later on revealed that they considered the Antioch group to be nonconforming innovators. Very fortunately it was Barnabas who went on a visit to the Antioch church. This generous-souled man had eyes to see the spirit of Jesus working in different and unusual ways. Barnabas mingled with the Antioch Christians. He went to church, and he "saw the grace of God."

The great Augustine once said, "Where Christ is, there is the church." We forward the cause of Christ when we have eyes to see Him working in unusual ways and give encouragement to the fresh, new releases of the energies of the grace of God.

Barnabas, the Generous, Gave a Second Chance to a Man Who Failed. The particular case was that of John Mark. John Mark got as far as Perga. It was all well enough going over to the island of Cyprus, for Cyprus was beautiful to look upon and the climate was moderate. Cyprus was delightful. Indeed, Cyprus is one of those lovely islands which, because they are off the beaten track of travelers, have been largely missed. John Mark enjoyed Cyprus well enough. But Perga on the mainland was utterly different. There John Mark was confronted with the malaria-ridden swamps of lower Asia Minor. There was heat and there was thick humidity. There was heavy going on the roads. And there was danger. One of these reasons or all of them made John Mark turn back. He went to Antioch.

After a very dangerous and painful campaign in Asia Minor, Paul went back to Antioch. In due time Paul would take Barnabas and start off on another western campaign. Barnabas wanted to take John Mark. Paul would not take the man who had turned back. Paul and Barnabas separated; Paul took Silas and Barnabas took John Mark. The sequel to that story came the day that Paul magnanimously allowed that Barnabas was right and wrote from Rome, "Take Mark, and bring him with thee: for he is useful to me for ministering" (II Timothy 4:11).

It was generous Barnabas, who would give a man who had failed a second chance, who saved John Mark. Can it be true that in doing so Barnabas also is responsible for giving us the gospel of Mark? Had John Mark been deserted perhaps he, in turn, would have deserted the church. Who knows? Certainly in saving Mark he saved the man who wrote the vivid foundational gospel which bears his name.

Time may reveal that we are in debt to Barnabas for both Paul and Mark, with all that they were, all that they did, and all that they wrote.

Barnabas belonged to the Jerusalem group of Jesus' disciples who had been the object of Saul's murderous heresy-hunting campaign. Yet it is Barnabas who warmly welcomes Saul to his own personal friendship and who commends Saul to the people of the church.

Then Generous, Sharing Barnabas Was a Man Filled with the Spirit of Jesus. It is exactly that which is said of Barnabas. "He was a good man, filled with the Holy Spirit and of faith." That is the spiritual life. When the spirit of genuineness, the spirit of faith in other men, the spirit of appreciation of Jesus working in unusual ways, the spirit of forgiveness and the second chance—when that is the spirit of a man because Jesus lives in his mind, that is spirituality. That is having the spirit of Christ.

When the spirit which was in Barnabas prevails we shall

not fail to find appropriate ways by which all men can share in the experience of all that is good. A man like Barnabas has no concern for imposing a particular pattern of life on the world. He goes far deeper than that. He releases the very spirit of Jesus Christ, and such a man will find different ways at different times and in different settings by which he will live at his highest by giving his best.

No wonder they gave to Joseph the nickname "Bar-Nabas," "Son of Consolation," "Son of Encouragement." Some author has described these sons of Consolation,—these choice men filled with the spirit of Jesus Christ, in the following lines:

"What was his creed? I do not know his creed.
I only know that here below
He walked the common road, lifted many a load,
Lightened the task, brightened the day
For others toiling on a weary way:
This his only meed. I do not know his creed.

"What was his creed? I never heard him speak
Of visions rapturous, of Alpine peak,
Of doctrine or dogma, new or old.
But this I know: He was forever bold
To stand alone; to meet the challenge of each new day;
To live the truth so far as he could see—the truth that
    ever makes men free.

"His creed?
I care not what his creed.
Enough that never yielded he to greed,
But helped his brother in his daily need,
Plucked many a thorn, planted many a flower,
Glorified the service of each hour,
Had faith in God, himself and follow men.
Perhaps he never thought in terms of creed.
I only know he lived a life in deed."

XVIII

SAUL OF TARSUS

The Decision To Obey

"I was not disobedient unto the heavenly vision."—ACTS 26:19.

THE city of Damascus is one of the oldest surviving cities of the world. Its history goes back through known history into the dim, unrecorded region of legend. While other cities have had their days and ceased to be, Damascus yet flourishes, with a population of some 250,000 people. It is situated on a plain that is over two thousand feet above sea level, a plain that passes into a great desert to the east and the south. Damascus is the center of a very fertile area, made fertile by the river Barada, the ancient Abana, which flows from the Anti-Lebanons. That is the clear-water stream which Naaman was sure was so superior to the Jordan. The Barada makes the region of Damascus fertile and lovely. One ancient Persian said of it, "Damascus is a diamond in a setting of pearls."

Damascus was the home of a considerable group of the disciples of Jesus, disciples who had evidently migrated from the region of Jerusalem. Saul of Tarsus, the Pharisee, on his own initiative, but with the approval of the Sanhedrin, was on his way to bring these renegade Jews back in chains to Jerusalem to stand trial.

Saul of Tarsus was well equipped as a heresy-hunter. He was a well-educated Pharisee. He was both a Roman and a Jew, born a Roman citizen and learned in Jewish history and law. His own home, Tarsus, was "no mean city," an educational center, where he learned Greek and was introduced to philosophy. As a youth, Saul went to the famous school of Gamaliel, at Jerusalem, where he advanced in proficiency as a student of all that was Jewish. His zeal for the temple and the law knew no bounds. When Stephen was stoned to death by mob action—really lynching—Saul stood by and gave his approval.

Saul had tasted blood and was out to kill. He gathered some similar spirits about him and marched for Damascus, fully persuaded in his own mind that he ought to hunt down and exterminate the heretical disciples of Jesus. Very likely he took the shortest and swiftest route across Samaria, skirted the Lake of Galilee, and pushed across Syria. At noonday, on the open road, with the sun ablaze in the Syrian sky, Saul was stricken to the earth in an experience that changed him and changed the course of his life. He not only made a decision that meant an immortal destiny for himself, he made a decision that changed the course of history. We cannot contemplate our situation in the fellowship of a modern church without our thinking threading its way back to that destiny-making decision of Saul of Tarsus on the Damascus road. Said he, "I was not disobedient to the heavenly vision."

The Experience of Saul of Tarsus on the Syrian Road Was a Great Spiritual Revelation. When Saul's physical eyes were blinded, the eyes of his spirit were opened to a heavenly vision of the Lord Jesus Christ.

Such a vision came to John the Baptist when he said, "I have need to be baptized of thee, and comest thou to me?" Such a vision came to Philip when as he said, "We have found him, of whom Moses in the law and the prophets did write, Jesus of Nazareth." Such a vision came to the woman of Samaria when she said, "Come, see a man that told me all things that ever I did. Is not this the Christ?" Such a vision came to Peter at Cæsarea Philippi when he said, "Thou art the Christ, the son of the living God." Such a vision came to the centurion at the cross—an experience reinterpreted in fiction in Lloyd C. Douglas' great novel, *The Robe,* when he said, "Truly this was the Son of God." Now that vision came to Saul of Tarsus, and he said, "Lord," for the eyes of his spirit had seen Jesus as He really is.

When a man has a vision of Jesus like that of Saul of Tarsus it does something to the man. It makes the man conscious of his sinfulness. A man cannot come into such a pure and refined presence without being conscious of the sharp contrast between the excellence of Jesus and his own faultiness. That happened to Peter in the boat on the Lake of Galilee. Peter really saw Jesus that day, and he said, "Depart from me, for I am a sinful man, O Lord." As a matter of fact, Peter didn't want to lose Jesus at all. It is language pushed to the extreme in an attempt to say, "I am so sinful that I have no right to be near thee, Lord, but I desire thee to deal with me and cure me of my sin."

I watched a man examining a fine piece of very thin cloth. It was to be used in a garment being made for a stately occasion. He held that piece of cloth against the sunlight that was streaming in through the window. In that sunlight he saw a flaw that could not be seen in the dimness of the room. That is what happens when any life really gets into the presence of Jesus. The flaws that are almost virtues in the dim light of our human standards are seen for what they are. That happened to Saul of Tarsus. By his own Pharisaic standards, he thought that "he ought to do many things." Later he was ashamed of them, saying, "I am not meet to be called an apostle, because I persecuted the church of God" (I Corinthians 15:9). In the presence of Jesus Saul of Tarsus saw that he was murderously injuring his fellow sons of God. He said of himself for all that, "Christ Jesus came into the world to save sinners; of whom I am chief" (I Timothy 1:15). The revelation of Jesus to the spirit of men has always two elements. It is not only a revelation of the beauty of Jesus. It is also a revelation of the ugliness of the man's own sinfulness. When that happens to a man, when

135

he knows that he a sinner has met the Saviour of sinners—that is a revelation that is full of hope.

The Experience of Saul of Tarsus Meant a Revolt. It was a revolt against a mistaken allegiance that had made him cruel and destructive.

Just as the revelation was two-sided, so the revolt was two-sided. Saul revolted against the institutions that had misled him. By the same token he transferred his allegiance to the Person he had met. He said, "Lord, what wilt thou have me to do?"

Perhaps the change in allegiance in the soul of Saul of Tarsus can be traced back, in part, to what he saw in the face of Stephen. Stephen's face, when he was being murdered, shone like the face of an angel, and as Jesus had done, Stephen prayed for his killers. A Spanish painter has attempted to portray what very likely happened in the soul of Saul of Tarsus that day. Saul is standing by as Stephen dies. The rage of the temple doctors is plainly visible on their faces. But on the face of Saul of Tarsus there is portrayed melancholy bewilderment. Saul had seen something. It is a strange fact of human nature that sometimes when a man begins to doubt the rightness of his course of action, he begins to whip himself into more vigorous behavior in that very direction. Perhaps Saul of Tarsus went away in a spirit like that.

The conversion on the Syrian roadway may have been sudden only in the sense that the flashing noonday light was sudden. It is easily possible that Saul was prepared in soul for just such a thing. In any event, the soul of Saul revolted, and he changed his allegiance to the authority of the Temple and the Sanhedrin to allegiance to the Lordship of Jesus. It was a clean-cut break with the past. It was another prodigal saying, "I will arise and go to my Father."

The Experience of Paul Was a Remaking of His Life. Indeed, it was from his first-hand, immediate experience of

Jesus that the apostle later says, "I know whom I have believed" (II Timothy 1:12); and "If any man is in Christ, he is a new creature: the old things are passed away; behold, they are become new" (II Corinthians 5:17).

The Old Testament tells of this remake of life in the picture of the potter and the clay in Jeremiah 18. The marred vessel is recast into another and better vessel, for it was to be remade according to the mind of the potter. In that vivid illustration it is well to remember always that clay is clay and souls are souls. It is the majestic and also the terrible prerogative of man to defy the purpose of the divine Potter. He also has the prerogative of desiring to be remade by God. Then the miracle happens.

John Masefield has related that for a long time he wished to portray in poetry the picture of a great conversion—the remaking of a man by the grace of God. That desire was realized in what is accepted as one of the great poems of our generation, *The Everlasting Mercy*. The central character of the poem is Saul Kane. Saul Kane is a drinking, carousing prize fighter. After a very gory ring fight, in which he knows he has fought for a lie, he goes again to the tavern to spend the night in a drinking bout. As was her custom, a little Quaker lady, Miss Bourne, visits the place to suggest to such men that there is a God with whom they must one day reckon. She speaks to Saul Kane. The drunken prize fighter is rude and rough in his reply.

> " 'Saul Kane,' she said, 'when next you drink,
>   Do me the gentleness to think
>   That every drop of drink accursed
>   Makes Christ within you die of thirst,
>   That every dirty word you say
>   Is one more flint upon His way,
>   Another thorn about His head,
>   Another mock by where He tread,
>   Another nail, another cross.
>   All that you are is that Christ's loss.' "

Who can describe the dealing of the spirit of God with a human soul? "The wind bloweth where it listeth, and thou hearest the sound thereof, but knowest not whence it cometh, and whither it goeth: so is every one that is born of the Spirit" (John 3:8). So it is with Saul Kane. The Quaker lady goes out. Then Saul Kane goes out. He walks in the night alone, but not alone, for God is near, God's spirit is working in him. The divine Potter has His hand on the willing human clay. Says Saul Kane:

> " 'The water's going out to sea
> And there's a great moon calling me;
> But there's a great sun calls the moon,
> And all God's bells will carol soon
> For joy and glory and delight
> Of someone coming home tonight.'
> Out into darkness, out to night,
> My flaring heart gave plenty light,
> So wild it was there was no knowing
> Whether the clouds or stars were blowing

> "And in my heart the drink unpriced,
> The burning cataracts of Christ.
> I did not think, I did not strive,
> The deep peace burnt my me alive;
> The bolted door had broken in,
> I knew that I had done with sin.
> I knew that Christ had given me birth
> To brother all the souls on earth." *

Saul Kane walks on and on until the morning finds him in a field beside a plowman, and there in the furrow he prays. By the hand of the divine Potter he is remade. He is a new creature.

Saul of Tarsus Becomes Paul the Apostle with a Sense of Divine Responsibility. Something happened that changed the course of human history when Paul said to his new-

---

* From "The Everlasting Mercy," by John Masefield. Used by permission of the publishers, The Macmillan Co., New York.

found Lord, "What wilt thou have me to do?" That was a decision with a destiny involved—a destiny not only for Paul, but for humanity. The outreach of that world-shaking event on the Damascus road is seen in every humble chapel in remote villages, in every schoolhouse in the plains where children are taught by weekday and a devoted farmer preaches to his neighbors on Sunday, in every church in town and city, in every great cathedral of Europe and America, in every Christian college, and in all the vast missionary programs of all the churches the world over. What a decision and what a destiny!

What Paul experienced and what Paul did has been repeated in the lives of like-minded men ever since. In America there is no more vivid, romantic and apostolic presentation of that than the life and work of Russell H. Conwell. When the Civil War was under way it found Russell Conwell, one year of work completed at Yale College, at Readville, Massachusetts. There he enlisted and undertook to enlist others. He was given the rank of captain. A young boy, Johnny Ring, was determined to go with Captain Conwell and he became the captain's personal attendant. The scene changed to the South. In North Carolina, at Newport River, Pickett's men had driven Captain Conwell's men across the wooden bridge, while the captain was about on duty. Johnny Ring remembered the captain's golden sword. It was the sword which was given to Captain Conwell at Springfield, and it always hung on the pole of his tent. Johnny Ring kept it polished. When Johnny Ring remembered that the sword was back in the tent on the ground now occupied by Pickett's men he dashed back over the wooden bridge, in among the Confederate soldiers, and reached the tent. He was on his way back, on the bridge, carrying the sword, when he was noticed. Now the bridge was ablaze. The lad fought his way among timbers and through flames. The Confederate captain slipped into the open and ordered "cease fire," and voices called to Johnny Ring to drop into the river and that he would be safe on either side. In the noise he could not hear. He reached the end of the bridge where the Massachusetts' men found him terribly burned. In hospital he lived three days, and his last words were, "Will you tell the captain that I saved his sword?"

The devotion of Johnny Ring had a grand sequel. A little later Captain Conwell, then Colonel Conwell, was severely wounded in the battle of Kenesaw Mountain, in Georgia. He was unconscious when rescued, and revived in hospital. That was Russell Conwell's Damascus Road. He met his Lord, and, like Paul, said, "What wilt thou have me to do?" Years later, Dr. Conwell said:

"When I stood beside the body of John Ring and realized he died for me I made a vow that has formed my life. I vowed that from then on I would not only live my life, but that I would live the life of John Ring as well. From that moment I have worked sixteen hours a day—eight for John Ring and eight for myself. Every morning I look at his sword, or, if I am away from home, I think of this sword and vow anew the accomplishment of sixteen hours' daily toil. It was through John Ring's sacrifice that I became a Christian. It did not come immediately, but it came before the war was over and it came through faithful Johnny Ring." *

It has been recorded that Russell Conwell earned $10,-000,000 during his lifetime by lecturing. Yet he died a poor man. That is, he was poor in the sense that Jesus was poor, who became poor that we through His poverty might become rich. Dr. Conwell erected a great church, the Baptist Temple of Philadelphia, where he ministered to over 3000

* From an article in the *Philadelphia Record* of Dec. 7, 1925, written just after the death of Dr. Russell H. Conwell.

members. He built Temple University, which numbers 10,000 students in its classrooms and has provided education for young people running into hundreds of thousands. He built three hospitals.

At last the physical strength of Russell Conwell gave way. He was lying in one of his own hospitals, when he wrote the lines that are the best possible record of his life. They were the last lines he ever wrote. They were published in the front pages of Philadelphia newspapers. He called the lines "My Prayer." Now they adorn the wall of the Baptist Temple, Philadelphia:

"I ask not for a larger garden,
    But for finer seeds.
I ask not for a more distant view,
    But for a clearer vision of the hills between.
I ask not to do more deeds,
    But more effective ones.
I ask not for a longer life,
    But for a more efficient one and for the present hour.

"I want to plant more,
    Proclaim more;
Tell the story of Jesus
    In clearer form;
I want the world to be more wise,
    And also more glad because I was used.

"May some oak say,
    'I grew stronger';
May some lily say,
    'I grew purer';
May some fountain say,
    'I threw the clear water higher.'

"May some good book be read;
May some good friendship be made;
May my total influence tell for righteousness,
Without an unnecessary tear."

Paul was not without a vision of just that sort of outreach

141

of the Christian message when he undertook to capture the city of Rome itself for his Lord. He met Jesus on the Damascus Road. His Lord said:

"I have appeared unto thee for this purpose, to make thee a minister and a witness both of those things which thou hast seen and of those things in the which I shall appear unto thee: Delivering thee from the people and from the Gentiles, unto whom now I send thee. To open their eyes and to turn them from darkness to light, and from the power of Satan unto God."

To Agrippa Paul said "Whereupon, O king Agrippa, I was not disobedient unto the heavenly vision. . . . King Agrippa, believest thou?"

The vision of the kingdom as Paul saw it reached the afflicted girl in the streets of Philippi—a demented child used by her owners to make profit, and it reached kings and Cæsar's household. Across the ages his clear voice rings, speaking to all men of every station in all lands everywhere:

"Let this mind be in you, which was also in Christ Jesus; Who, being in the form of God, thought it not robbery to be called equal with God: but made himself of no reputation, and took upon him the form of a servant, and was made in the likeness of men: and being found in fashion as a man, he humbled himself, and became obedient unto death, even the death of the cross. Wherefore God also hath highly exalted him, and given him a name which is above every name: that in the name of Jesus every knee should bow, of things in heaven, and things in earth, and things under the earth: and that every tongue should confess that Jesus Christ is Lord, to the glory of God the Father" (Philippians 2: 5-11).

We live in the fellowship of and we struggle as a toiler with Paul when we say,

"Be Thou my Vision, O Lord of my heart;
Naught be all else to me, save that Thou art—
Thou my best thought, by day and by night,
Waking or sleeping, Thy presence my light.

"High King of heaven, my victory won,
May I reach heaven's joys, O bright heaven's Sun!
Heart of my own heart, whatever befall,
Still be my vision, O Ruler of all." *

* From an Old Irish hymn, translated by Mary Byrne, and versified by Eleanor Hull. No. 307, *The New Church Hymnal*, D. Appleton-Century Co., Inc., New York City.